THE WORKS OF
GILBERT *of* HOYLAND

Translated and introduced by

LAWRENCE C. BRACELAND SJ

GILBERT OF HOYLAND

Volume One

ON THE
SONG OF SONGS I

CISTERCIAN FATHERS SERIES : NUMBER FOURTEEN

Gilbert, abbot of Swineshead, Holland, "Lincolnshire.

Sermons on the Song of Songs, I

CISTERCIAN PUBLICATIONS, INC.
KALAMAZOO, MICHIGAN 49008
1978

BS 1485
G49
vol. 1

The translator and publishers are grateful
for the help and encouragement of
The Canada Council
The Research Board of the University of Manitoba
Dr. H. E. Kane SJ, Rector of St Paul's College

The translation here presented is based on the edition of Jean Mabillon,
Milan, Gnocchi, reprint of 1852.

Original Latin title:
Sermones in Canticum Salomonis ab eo loco ubi B. Bernardus
morte praeventus desiit.

Available in Europe and the Commonwealth from
A. R. Mowbray & Co Ltd.
Saint Thomas House, Becket Street
Oxford OX1, 1SG, England

Library of Congress Cataloging in Publication Data

Gilbert, Abbot of Swineshead, Holland, Lincolnshire.
   On the Song of songs I.

   (Cistercian fathers series ; no. 14) (The works of
Gilbert of Hoyland ; v. 1)
   Bibliography: p. 193
   Includes index.
   1. Bible. O.T. Song of Solomon—Criticism, interpre-
tation. I. Title. II. Series: Gilbert, Abbot of
Swineshead, Holland, Lincolnshire. Sermones in Canticum
Salomonis ab eo loco ubi B. Bernardus morte praeventus
desiit. English ; v. 1.
BS1485.G49   223'.9'006   77-23026
ISBN 0-87907-414-0

Book design by Gale Akins
Typeset at Humble Hills Graphics; Kalamazoo, Michigan 49004
Printed in the United States of America

For George Bernard Cardinal Flahiff
of the Congregation of Saint Basil

Cui dono lepidum novum libellum
Gilberti sophia styloque bellum?
Bernarde tibi, qui nec aestimabis
Nugas esse meas meum libellum
Ex aevo medio probe politum.
Tu vero sapiens, amore doctus
Jam regis populum Dei modernum
Doctis vocibus atque amore prisco.
Quare Doctor habe novum libellum,
Quare Praesul ames tuum libellum,
Qui cantare velit divinum amorem,
Delectum Dominum per omne saeclum.

CONTENTS

INTRODUCTION

T O ENCOUNTER a person who makes holiness attractive is
an enviable experience. Such a person was Gilbert of Hoyland,
abbot of Swineshead in Lincolnshire, one of the early
Cistercian authors who shed so much light on the spiritual
life of the twelfth century. These early Cistercians have become well
known to English readers especially through *The Mystical Theology of
St Bernard* by Etienne Gilson and *The Love of Learning and the Desire
for God* by Jean Leclercq. Gilson examines the independence and com-
plementarity of the two dominant stars, St Bernard and William of
St Thierry, and points to three secondary stars in the background,
St Aelred of Rievaulx, Gilbert of Hoyland and Isaac of Stella, who
'may serve to designate the three founders and principal interpreters of
what we may fairly call the Cistercian school'. Gilson considers remarkable the 'similarity of intellectual formation and tastes . . . in men of
so diverse an origin'. This similarity Jean Leclercq largely accounts for
by explaining the formation, sources, and fruits of monastic culture,
for these early Cistercians shared the same devotion to heaven, love of
sacred learning, traditional spirituality, and liberal studies.[1]

We do not lack contemporary and modern lives, critical editions and
penetrating studies of Bernard and Aelred, Isaac of Stella and William
of St Thierry, but Gilbert of Hoyland has been less well served. He is
best remembered as the abbot who 'continued' the Sermons of Bernard
on the Canticle of Canticles, in one of which he gave a deeply moving,
personal eulogy of Aelred. Gilbert's sermons, treatises and letters
were published by Mabillon in an edition substantially reliable, according to Fr Edmond Mikkers, and subsequently reprinted by Migne.
Though Gilbert deserves a modern critical edition to match the hand-
some new editions of St Bernard and John of Ford, and to complete a
continuous series on the Canticle by three great Cistercians, this translation has been made from the adequate and available edition

3

of Mabillon.[2]

The brief details of Gilbert's life and work were judiciously presented by Fr Edmond Mikkers, editor of *Cîteaux*. From his dissertation on Gilbert's Sermons, we have two published excerpts in *Cîteaux* and an article on Gilbert in the *Dictionnaire de Spiritualité* by Fr M. Jean Vuong-dinh-Lam, now a Cistercian abbot in Vietnam. Fr. Pierre Miquel contributed a brief study on the characteristics of Gilbert's religious experience. Fr Mikkers concludes his double article with a clear statement of the need for further research into the work of Gilbert:

> If up to the present [1963] his theological and mystical teaching has been scarcely explored, this may be attributed not only to general ignorance of monastic theology but also to the rather difficult style of Gilbert's latinity. In his work many chapters remain to be considered, for example questions on Christology, on his teaching and practice of the virtues, but especially on the mystical life and union with God. Not only is he a faithful imitator of St Bernard but also a true witness of the so-called monastic theology as it flourished in the monasteries of England.[3]

Further study is needed on Gilbert's work, written with the insight and love with which, for example, the life and writings of St Aelred have been presented. Such a study would explore Gilbert's anthropology and psychology, philosophy and theology, and his use of Scripture.

GILBERT AND THREE EARLY CISTERCIANS

Gilbert became known not by the name of his monastery in Swineshead but by the name of Hoyland or Holland, the fenland around the Wash on the east coast of England. We know neither the date of his birth nor his country of origin, although authors have claimed him for England, Scotland, and Ireland. From the beginning he is listed as a monk of Clairvaux. Whatever his country of origin and the monastery he entered, Gilbert joined the Cistercians in the lifetime of St Bernard of Clairvaux. We can trace his relationship with Bernard and Aelred and with a third early Cistercian, the impressive but less well known Roger, abbot of Byland. Roger's close connection with Gilbert is sufficient reason to include his only extant identified work, *Lac Parvulorum,* with this translation of the writings of Gilbert.[4]

Gilbert and Bernard

Abbot Gilbert died in 1172, nineteen years after the death of the abbot Bernard of Clairvaux. In recording his death at the monastery of L'Arrivour, near Troyes in modern France, the Chronicler of Clairvaux notes Gilbert's distinction in composing his Sermons on the Canticle after the manner of Blessed Bernard. Derived ultimately from the Chronicler, the following brief but luminous account is appended to a manuscript of Gilbert's Sermon:

> *The reverend, distinguished, most devout and most learned Father, Dom Gilbert, formerly abbot of Hoyland, in England, composed the sermons contained in this volume on the Canticle of Canticles, following with great distinction and learning the manner and style of Blessed Bernard.*[5]

Three passages in Gilbert indicate his relationship with Bernard. He read and reverenced Bernard's writing and may have heard the saint in person. Explaining why he refrains from comment on a passage already 'developed at length and with accuracy', Gilbert pays tribute to Bernard: 'Whether the author be the more remarkable for learning or for eloquence I know not, but the matter in the pages of his homilies it ill becomes me to turn over for discussion, pardon me, even with my little finger'. In a later sermon Gilbert avoids the repetition of Bernard's comment and substitutes comments of his own: 'It is good to linger among ointments but since enough has been said elsewhere about their various kinds, let us now briefly distinguish the various ways of anointing'. In an earlier sermon Gilbert quotes from memory an interpretation of an 'eloquent and learned man', apparently Bernard, but Gilbert does not hesitate to propose a different interpretation: 'I remember the explanation of an eloquent and learned man when treating of this passage: . . . . What he said suited the occasion well enough; he directed his comment to the advantage of his audience. To me however . . . .'[6] We shall return later to the words of the Chronicler and to Gilbert's relationship with Bernard.

Gilbert and Aelred

Gilbert seems to have had time to assimilate the Cistercian spirit, to grow to the stature of abbot, and to become eligible for appointment to Swineshead some time before the year 1150, perhaps as early as 1147.

If he had entered Clairvaux even shortly before 5 March 1132, he could well have left Clairvaux with the founding monks who at that date settled Rievaulx in Yorkshire.[7] This would account for his deep insight into and friendship for Aelred (1110–67), who entered Rievaulx from the Court of King David of Scotland about the year 1134.[8] Aelred became master of novices at Rievaulx in 1142, was abbot of Revesby some fifteen miles north of Swineshead, 1143–47, and abbot of Rievaulx from 1147 until his death on 11 January 1167. One of Aelred's first acts as abbot of Rievaulx was to dispatch a contingent of monks, one of whom may have been Gilbert, to aid the Savigniacs at Swineshead in adopting and following the Cistercian observance.[9]

An extended sojourn together under the same roof would account for the quality of Gilbert's eulogy of Aelred, for 'Gilbert of Hoiland and Jocelin of Furness give the salient traits of Ailred's character more clearly than Walter Daniel does'.[10] In his eulogy shortly after he received news of Aelred's death, Gilbert writes from personal acquaintance:

> I remember how often, when some one in his audience rudely interrupted the course of his instruction, he stopped speaking until the other had fully exhausted his breath. When the gushing torrent of untimely speech had ebbed away, he would resume his interrupted discourse with the same calmness with which he waited, for he both spoke and kept silent as the occasion demanded. He was quick to listen, slow to speak, but not slow to anger. How can he be described as slow to anger? Rather I would say he was not even in the race![11]

Continuing his praise of Aelred as the 'honeycomb overflowing with honey', Gilbert gives the substance and significance of the little *doctor mellifluus*, later to be conferred on Bernard and here personified in Aelred, the Bernard of the North.[12] Then with obvious allusion to Aelred's *Spiritual Friendship,* composed about the year 1160, Gilbert proceeds to comment on the distinction between 'friends' and 'dearly beloved' in texts spoken by the Lord. In the context Gilbert implies that Aelred was the personification of friendship and 'the most dearly beloved'.[13]

Gilbert and Roger of Byland

Aelred received the last rites from Roger of Byland, who also preached his funeral oration. Unlike Aelred, who with the exception of some four years at Revesby spent all his Cistercian life at Rievaulx, Roger was obliged to move to many different sites. The monastery he entered, a daughter house of Savigny in France, was founded at Tulketh on 4 July 1124, and was then moved in 1127 to Furness, that mother of many daughters including both Byland and Swineshead. 'Roger was one of the twelve monks who in 1134 (1135) set out with their abbot Gerald . . . to establish a house at Calder' in Cumberland, where he became a subcellarer. 'When that foundation was destroyed by the Scots and the community returned to take shelter at Furness', they were 'turned adrift and forced to take shelter in Yorkshire'. The community settled at Hood in September 1138, at Old Byland in September 1142, at Stocking in 1147, and finally at New Byland on 30 October 1177.[14]

Roger became master of novices at Hood. Abbot Gerald had 'travelled to Savigny and at the General Chapter there in 1142, obtained release from the jurisdiction of Furness but on his way home from the Chapter died at York. Roger was then elected abbot of Byland in an unusual way. As novice master, Roger was explaining to his one novice the observance of the Savigniac Order. Suddenly and unexpectedly the monks arrived, rushed towards him and seized him. Carrying him shoulder high in procession to the altar in the oratory, they chanted in a loud voice that he was their abbot in the name of the Trinity'. Continuing 'to rule Byland for the next fifty-four years', Roger was abbot during the moves from Hood to Old Byland to Stocking and finally to New Byland. One move was made because Byland had been located too close to Rievaulx; 'at each hour of the day and night, both abbeys heard each other's bells' to the confusion especially of the brethren working in the fields.[15]

The year 1147 was momentous for Savigny and her daughters, and not least in England. At the Savigniac General Chapter which began in Rheims on Trinity Sunday in the presence (and perhaps with the encouragement) of Pope Eugene III, once a monk of Clairvaux, the Savigniac Abbot General Serlo, thirteen French abbots, the abbot of Neath, the abbot of Quarr, and abbot Roger of Byland agreed to affiliate the Savigniac foundations with the family of Clairvaux. Then at the Cistercian General Chapter which began in September, Savigny and her thirty daughters, including three priories of nuns, were accepted into the Cistercian Order. The merger was first confirmed by Eugene III on 19 September 1147, and then more formally on 10 April 1148, by a bull in which all the English Savigniac foundations and filiations were mentioned by name, because opposition to union with Clairvaux continued in England, centered around abbot Peter of Furness.[16] Abbot Peter's forced resignation from the motherhouse of

Furness may have provided the opportunity for Gilbert's appointment to the daughter house of Swineshead.[17]

Roger was by now acquainted with Bernard of Clairvaux and with Abbot Serlo of Savigny. Abbot Serlo had 'ordered a visitation of the English Savigniac houses and in 1148 his deputy, the abbot of Quarr, decided that Roger should take responsibility for the new foundation' at Wensleydale in the valley of the Ure.[18] Roger must have been responsible for the move of this new daughter house from Fors to Jervaulx in 1150, and he relied entirely on Bernard's 'influence to smooth over the difficulties raised by this matter', at the General Chapter. 'Later when the rapid expansion of Byland and the resulting burden of administration moved Roger to seek resignation from office, he asked the advice and support of Bernard, who counselled him to continue to govern his house "with industry and discretion" '. Roger had pleaded that he was too incompetent to rule his house any longer because he was worn out by weakness and age—he was to rule for four decades after Bernard's death! Bernard also pointed out that Roger's successors could not support and retain the lands and possessions which Roger had acquired in his time.[19] At this time or somewhat later, 'Roger also confided his intention to Gilbert of Swineshead', and received from Gilbert the answers we have in his lengthy seventh treatise. In 1153 or 1154, a controversy arose between Furness and Savigny concerning the jurisdiction each claimed over Byland. Aelred of Rievaulx heard the case and drew up the document to decide the dispute in favor of Savigny. The document was signed with the seals of Gilbert and many other Cistercian abbots.[20]

Gilbert's seventh treatise (and perhaps his first treatise also) is addressed to Roger of Byland; Roger's only known extant work, *The Milk of Babes,* is addressed tantalizingly to G., as its editor noted, but, as Edmond Mikkers observes, it was almost certainly meant for Gilbert of Hoyland.[21] If this be so, we have from Roger a sketch of the young Gilbert, as we also have from Gilbert a sketch of the mature Roger. When C. H. Talbot published this vocation letter, he argued convincingly that Roger was the author and told Roger's story with humor and finesse, but was less concerned with Roger's appreciation of Gilbert and his attempt to win a desirable recruit for the Cistercian Order. As Roger suggests, Gilbert's idealism in the service of an earthly king could be turned to the service of the divine Majesty. His love of parents could be directed to the love of Christ in the Cistercian family. His strong self-will could be firmly guided towards the will of God. His love of wealth could be exchanged for the love of eternal treasure. Roger cautions Gilbert: 'Let not ambition for wealth delight you because your fathers possessed churches by hereditary right'. From Scripture Roger formulates and answers an objection of this young Samuel to the harsh life of the Cistercians: 'But weak am I and delicate. Because reared in royal purple, I am incapable of enduring a regime so harsh or a regime so burdensome'. Obviously anyone 'steeped in the literature of a pagan'—Roger means philosophy and literary style—did not need 'sparkling circumlocutions or polished sentences in the ornate style', but rather 'the milk of babes'. He needed a reminder of the four last things; he needed to love Mary the mother of mercy; he needed to realize that he was welcome among the Cistercians and that he shared a very large part in the heart of that strong spiritual father in God, Roger of Byland.

The writings of Gilbert and Roger show both their distinctive personalities and their common formation in Cistercian spirituality. Gilbert's writings also reflect the influence of Roger's letter to him. Gilbert is as aware as Bernard not only that beginners need 'the milk of babes' but also that the proficient need more solid food. Gilbert's vivid description of the ravages of disease in a monk's death recalls in a gentler way Roger's macabre account of the wanton's progress to disintegration. The commonplace of the harshness of externals in the Cistercian life both writers freely admit and set in its proper context. Gilbert, however, plays on the origin of the word Cistercian. Cis, the father of Saul, is one whose name means 'harsh' and his name signifies not the harsh externals of the Cistercian life but any monk in office who becomes a 'harshtercian' father to his sons.[22] Gilbert's own vocation letter, to a scholarly Adam not otherwise identified, shows more delicacy and understanding towards a man trained in literature and in philosophy, for Gilbert knew from experience that this was a valuable discipline for disciples of the Lord; yet he was as blunt as Roger in his direct approach to Adam.[23] Identical arguments against Roger's resignation appear both in Bernard and in Gilbert's seventh treatise, where also his advice 'reveals the love and reverence with which Roger was held by his friends . . . the great material and spiritual prosperity which attended his government and the considerable pains he took to avoid involving himself in cares alien to his office'.[24]

SWINESHEAD

Roger of Byland, that unambitious man and born leader of men, the friend of Bernard, Serlo, and Aelred, was deeply interested in the vocation, formation, and career of that equally self-effacing man, Gilbert, abbot of Swineshead. Swineshead Abbey, founded 1 February 1135, was endowed, not richly, by Robert de Gresley and his son, Albert, with two hundred forty acres, of which much was fenland, and 'in the same vill, with some mills and fisheries and a moiety of the church of Cotgrave, Nottinghamshire'.[25] On the death of Robert Gresley in 1166, his widow Hawyse added to the endowment. 'Other benefactors were Stephen, earl of Brittany, Robert d'Arcy, Alan de Croun, Gilbert of Ghent, Henry de Longchamp, Simon, earl of Montford and many of less note'.[26] Another benefactor was William of Roumara, earl of Lincoln. Over the years benefactions continued.[27]

One might be tempted to compare the site and endowment of Swineshead unfavorably with other sites already mentioned: Clairvaux, Rievaulx, Furness, and Byland. In fact, many of the Savigniac sites in England were considered poor in all things save the quality of their monks.[28] The Savigniacs who bade farewell to Furness for Swineshead were leaving an abbey still youthful but situated in a narrow valley near Barrow-in-Furness at the extremity of the Furness peninsula in the modern county of Cumbria. The abbey would develop 'great estates with prosperous sheepwalks and corngranges and remained wealthy to the end'.[29] The monks came to lowland and fenland in a district called Hoyland which had obvious similarities to the Netherlands and was not without future promise. They would have opportunities for sheep-grazing and cattle-raising. They would be challenged to reclaim the fenland from river and sea, despite the ever-present danger of floodings and the ominous whistling of the wind from northeast or northwest.[30] At Swineshead the founders from Furness were joined by a contingent of Cistercians from Rievaulx, and the practical link between Savigny, Clairvaux, and Rievaulx may have been that extraordinarily practical and spiritual mover of monks, Roger of Byland.

Abbot Gilbert

Several passages in Gilbert's sermons suggest that he did not accompany John, the founder abbot, and his monks from Furness but arrived from elsewhere to become John's immediate successor. As abbot, Gilbert praises his monks for their understanding of prayer and their frequent and fervent practice for which he takes no credit. 'I have frequently found you well versed in pursuits of this sort. I cannot boast that I have engendered these affections in you, though I rejoice to have found you in them. And if I have not formed these interests in you, may I at least encourage you in them!' Alluding to his superiors who sent him to

Swineshead, he speaks of the mantle of office as the heavy burden of the care of souls and the anxiety of temporal administration: 'Woe to me that the city watchmen found me, that they thought they found something in me deserving of such a burden'. Scattered throughout his work are many lessons about such watchmen: teachers, preachers, prelates, abbots and their audiences. His ideal abbot is personified in Aelred of Rievaulx and Roger of Byland.[31]

Gilbert's Audience

Only in three sermons and in two treatises does Gilbert use the plural of address throughout.[32] Thirteen sermons show only the singular of address, to which may be added another four with one or two words or one or two sentences in the plural inserted for the occasion and easily detachable. The remaining thirty sermons have singulars and plurals mainly for variety and to bring home the point to each individual auditor. The individual is the faithful soul, *fidelis anima,* or the human soul, *humana anima,* or the individual as *sponsa,* feminine or masculine. The plurals often addressed to the brethren, *fratres,* are used in the wider sense for all souls seeking the Cistercian way and do not exclude the ladies.[33]

Sermons fifteen to twenty-two form a recognizable series which comments on Canticle 3:3-11, a natural unit in the Vulgate to be sung by the chorus in the Canticle. These sermons show that they were used for nuns and in the seventeenth sermon we become aware of the presence of young ladies, *adulescentulae,* perhaps servants or candidates for the cloister. Full of color, vivid imagination, and tender emotion, this group of sermons in some ways shows Gilbert at his best. In two beautiful passages we may notice the veiled advice to nuns on the choice of an expert in the word of God and how a spiritually dead monk is treated by his Cistercian mother.[34] A moving passage in a later sermon, on the little fig tree which first produced the sweet fruit of virginity and later the bitter fruit of repentance, shows Gilbert's own great heart and the greater heart of the Beloved. Though Gilbert knew this soul personally, he leaves us to guess the identity and the cloister of a soul restored to spiritual life as Lazarus was restored from the tomb and a contemporary of Aelred's nun of Watton.[35]

To what monastery or priory did these nuns belong? Though the Cistercians had not officially accepted the care of souls in general or of nuns who on their own initiative had adopted the Cistercian rule or practices, monks of the Savigniac family had assumed the care of nuns and continued this care even after their union with Cîteaux. Though this might have been true of Swineshead, in the absence of contemporary records the evidence suggests that these nuns were Gilbertines founded by Gilbert of Sempringham or nuns of some other foundation keen to adopt the rule and practice of Cîteaux.[36] Sempringham, founded by Gilbert of Sempringham, who tried vainly to have his many foundations affiliated with Clairvaux, was only about ten miles to the southwest of Swineshead (near Horbling on the modern map). The nuns were eager to receive Cistercian direction and guidance, and the practical Gilbert of Hoyland kept them in mind.[37]

The monks of Swineshead, including the founding monks from Furness, the contingent from Rievaulx, and new recruits, seem to have become numerous, for Gilbert speaks of 'this crowded gathering'. From the beginning he found that they 'applied themselves frequently and fervently in prayer'. Many a time he praises their avidity for contemplation: 'You urge me to lay down for you some rule for contemplating the Beloved and to give you a method for this discovery and vision', and later: 'I see that your readiness to listen is now enkindled anew. Your appetite has been whetted by the fragrance of the bride's ointments. Through some immoderate hunger you desire this theme to be added today . . . grant me a truce until morning'. Their mutual humility and their love of Christ he recognized and praised: 'Call to mind how you beg one another for the help of prayers, with what humble feelings, what earnest desires and what adjurations'. Finally, in a long and enviable picture of their daily life, Gilbert embraces all his community in an ideal presentation of the perfect Cistercian life.[38]

Gilbert does not shirk his duty to call attention to weakness and to suggest a cure often with wry humor and a dash of satire. On occasion, he tells us, some speak too harshly about their abbot or their brethren. A few waste time in idleness to the neglect of spiritual pursuits. Idlers do not follow the example of the ancient fathers in simplicity and love of solitude, while a few ludicrously abuse their sign language.[39] This reads like a chapter of faults. Gilbert's heartiest satire is reserved for some vain and ambitious individuals: Brother William who is flexing his ostrich wings to take flight to the court of a duke, the likely successors of Roger and their vanity and ambition, the pompous preacher and the niggardly bursar, the disaffected monk and the complaining nun.[40]

The receipt of a sermon, a treatise, or a letter from Gilbert must have been an exciting event. If we read him only for his spiritual content and for theological insights taken out of context—for example in the *index locupletissimus* of Mabillon—we may miss the vibrant man of his times, the monk toiling manually with his confrères at tasks of all kinds, and the humble but worthy bearer of the mantle of an abbot. If he was not a native of the fens of south Lincolnshire, we find him in his writings a naturalized citizen of the district of Hoyland, where he continued to plant the seed of the word in rich silt reclaimed from the ocean. Ruminating on the word after the Cistercian manner, he seasoned it with the salt of the sea. Once only, indirectly and pejoratively, does he mention swine, in connection with the prodigal returned to his father while the elder brother grunted. In his many references to birds and beasts, he seems to use Scripture with his own readings and observations rather than literal quotations from Isidore of Seville or from the bestiaries. In his first treatise, on the contemplation of heaven, he seems to be alluding to the *Confession* of the Archpoet (died 1165), a contemporary of Gilbert (died 1172).[41] Gilbert adapts to his own era the soldiering metaphor frequent in monastic writings, but the two living metaphors which move him most were derived, one from the site of his own monastery and the other from the allegory of love in the Canticle.

In explaining and adapting scriptural texts, Gilbert manifests his concern for all his monks with their assorted jobs around the monastery: the beekeeper with his helmet-shaped hives and his full honeycombs, the gardeners with many kinds of vegetable gardens, flowerplots and orchards, the chemist and the silversmith, the tailor and the chandler, the cobbler, the barber, and the baker, the fisherman tacking at sea, the irrigator and the well-digger, the hunter cocking one eye, the plowman, and the shepherd with his sheep and his dog. We should not forget the two nuns, one overburdened and creaking like a cart loaded with hay and the other bustling along like a proud carriage of the Lord. Nor should we neglect the bird-watcher charmed by the songster or awaiting migration. This world, all recorded in the Scriptures, was alive and well in Swineshead, to be recorded by Gilbert who forgot none of his little people, so admirable and so worthy of praise and sometimes so earthy and so comical.[42]

The monastic soldiering metaphor Gilbert deftly adapts to his text and to his time and place. Monks in the service of the divine Majesty must defend the city of God from enemies within and without. His commentary lets us hear echoes of encroachment on the border, border warfare, defence of the city by walls and ramparts, by towers and outworks against war within and war without, by the use of mail, helmets, shields, sword-play, and duelling.[43] By some literary historians Gilbert is considered a source in the development of the legend of the holy grail, not surprisingly, for the quest is practically a Cistercian re-creation.[44]

Acknowledging his debt to Alfred Pauphilet, Roger Sherman Loomis in 'The *"Queste del Saint Graal"*: Celtic Story-Patterns in Cistercian Allegory', finds in Gilbert the source of four developments in the legend. The name of Galahad, the Christ-knight, which is derived from the biblical Galaad or Gilead and means a 'mount of witness', is interpreted as a reference to Christ by Isidore of Seville, Walafrid Strabo, and the Venerable Bede. Gilbert asks in his twenty-third sermon: 'Who is this [Mount Gilead] but Christ, for on him all the testimonies of the prophets are piled and to him the prophets, John the Baptist, the heavenly Father and his own works bear witness'. In the same sermon, Professor Loomis finds the clue to an allegorical role played by fickle Fortune: 'She is, when bald, a personification of the Old Law . . . . After explaining that Mount Galaad signified Christ, [Gilbert] continued in this remarkable style':

> Do not fall from this mount if you are a hair. Why do you threaten to be separated from us and to be plucked from the flock of the remaining locks? Will your fall inflict baldness on the Church? She cannot suffer baldness for her hairs are all numbered. It was to the Synagogue that the threat was made by Isaiah: 'Instead of curled locks there will be baldness'. The locks of the Church [faithful souls] are curled, always recoiling to her head, encircling it in a friendly embrace, striving to enter the secrets of her head. Therefore her hairs do not tumble from but ascend to Mount Gilead, accumulating for their own imitation ever greater examples of Christ's works.

Loomis concludes that 'it is next to certain that this passage inspired the author of Perlesvaus'. He then credits Gilbert as the source of two further developments in the *Queste del Saint Graal,* for Gilbert 'equated in his second sermon the bed of Solomon with the cross of Christ', in the passage where he exclaims: 'A welcome little bed is the wood of your Cross!' Loomis concludes: 'This equation being accepted, it follows that Galahad, the Christ-Knight, was destined to lie upon the bed, and so he does later on the voyage to Sarras'. Finally in the sixteenth sermon of Gilbert, Loomis finds the origin of St Paul's sword of the word hanging from Galahad's side:

> Let 'the sword of the spirit' be 'versatile' in your grasp, a trusty servant in every task confronting you . . . Let the sword of the word be at your side, not in hiding . . . Gird it upon your thigh, that you may be powerful and prompt

both 'to encourage with sound doctrine' and to refute adversaries.

'The sword', comments Loomis with Pauphilet, 'which lay at the foot of the bed and which was destined for Galahad affords another extraordinary example of the author's practice of blending romantic motifs from the Matter of Britain with biblical themes and mystical interpretations'.

Gilbert was also fascinated by the restlessly changing natural world best known to the lowlander on either side of the North Sea, where from Roman times and before, man had fought for survival. Gilbert prays that the north wind with its desolating frost will alternate with the south wind with its consoling warmth. He understands the management of fresh water from streams, fountains, and wells and the need for dykes, channels, sluice-gates, and systems of irrigation to protect fresh water from the brine of the sea.[45] Subject to the seasons, the perils of the equinox, the perpetual ebb and flow of the tide, man's attempts to maintain the higher land and to reclaim the silt from both flash floods and ocean innundations make him restless and weary amid the changing but unwearied elements, until he cries out for peace at the end. The metaphor of the dyked ocean, never long absent in his writings, Gilbert used with startling effectiveness in his neglected sixth treatise. There 'the measureless ocean of divine Majesty' seeps drop by drop through the dyke of our humanity to be caught in the inebriating chalice which is Christ.

> Christ is at once inebriated and inebriating. He is the toastmaster and the chalice. He is at once the goblet and the wine, wine pure and wine mixed, for wisdom mixed wine in his mixing bowl. How sparkling you are, O inebriating mixing bowl! Sparkling indeed, radiant in truth, intoxicating with delight.

Gilbert's correspondent is to catch some precious drops in the navel-cup of his soul, so that he need never come again to Gilbert's well to drink.

> So let the navel of your soul be like a rounded mixing bowl, refined and purified and made fine and capacious by the scalpel of penance and discipline, that you may be filled to the brim and inebriated, that the verse may rightly be applied to you: 'Your navel is a rounded bowl which never lacks mixed wine'.[46]

The Writer Among His Monks

In the midst of the monks whom he observed, praised, and prayed for, and to whom his door was always open, Gilbert sighed now and then for fewer interruptions, for more leisure for contemplation and for precious moments to record his reflections. Though he manifests his sensitivity to the fenland site of his own abbey, he finds time to describe the more beautiful site of Byland (Stocking). For the garden of the bride he records the natural splendor of mountains and hills, the enchantment of a well-planned garden with its trees and flowers and the scent of aromatic plants.[47] Yet with St Paul he preferred to look up and ahead rather than to look back, except occasionally to the idealized past of the early Church, to her martyrs and her doctors.

Gilbert lived with his monks in the school of Christ, where he learned by experience and taught with discretion, providing milk for babes and solid food for the proficient. His textbooks were the Scriptures, the Rule of St Benedict, the Fathers who developed the traditions of monastic life, the liturgy, the natural environment, and the living community. He read and explained his textbooks with the conviction that the letter kills but the Spirit gives life, that the literal sense must be completed by the spiritual, the Old by the New Testament, prefigurements by the promised reality, the prophets and patriarchs by the Messiah. His reverence for the Rule of St Benedict is shown in two subtle ways: he prefers to paraphrase rather than to cite the Rule, except in one place where he refers to the Rule as a final argument introduced by *denique,* the word reserved for the unchallengeable argument of the Scriptures; yet he admits that the letter of the Rule is lifeless and uses to the full the liberating humanity of its famous final paragraph. Likewise, in his epistolary treatise to Roger of Byland, he expresses his admiration for and need to adapt 'the ancients, who transmitted to us their experience of religious life, for their authority is more ancient and their purity more perfect . . . . They were servants of their era, let us be servants of ours'.[48] While showing his admiration for Bernard, he realized that as Bernard adapted even the Scripture to the occasion for the benefit of his listeners, so could he. On the letter and the spirit of Cîteaux, could any passage better manifest Gilbert's psychological insight and warmth of heart than his words about a brother spiritually sick unto death? Could anyone speak more movingly about union of hearts in a community than Gilbert has done in explaining the parable of the pomegranate?

He has also left us a record of the ideal Cistercian life in describing a full day in the spiritual life of his community.[49]

THE WRITTEN WORD, SACRED AND PROFANE

Like the works of many monastic contemporaries, the works of Gilbert exhibit a familiarity with the pagan classics and an enviable style, always subordinated to his unwavering purpose of communicating his teaching and his enthusiasm for the ascetical life. In a spirited passage in defense of the writer of spiritual books, he begins with a quotation from Horace: 'Good it is if words be spoken but it is not less good if words be written, "for the word flies off beyond recall", unless it is captured in writing'.[50] A few other quotations and many reminiscences of Horace throw light on his meaning. Again, he satirizes ostentatious monks with classical allusions: 'Each of these characters you will recognize as a [swashbuckling] Thraso in gesture, an innkeeper in merrymaking, a [parasitical] Gnatho in a brawl. Each wishes to appear as a Cato in chapter, a Cicero in court, a Virgil among the poets'.[51] Seneca he quotes frequently, but as a philosopher. Though familiar with the classics, he had no doubt about the priority of the sacred page over the secular for a cleric or a monk: 'In the mouth of a cleric or of a monk, sacred literature is much more fitting than secular. Why do you wish to speak Egyptian in Jerusalem'?[52] Yet in all his writings, though he tended to hide her, his shy classical virgin peeps out unexpectedly through the veil of his pages to throw light on the bride of the Canticle.

His appreciation for literature and philosophy, which we gather from the vocation letter of Roger of Byland, is confirmed by Gilbert's own vocation letter to Adam, a scholarly young cleric not otherwise identified:

Not that I disparage erudition in the arts, a ready memory in liberal studies and a clear understanding, for on these depends the integrity of knowledge. For skill in the arts is valuable provided one uses them rightly, that is as a step and foothold where one does not stop and rest, but which one must use to rise to higher and holier and more interior mysteries of Wisdom, to those hidden and pleasant retreats and to the very light inaccessible which God inhabits.

That Gilbert includes philosophy among the steps leading to Wisdom, becomes clear in the same paragraph:

The tenuous and ambiguous knowledge of natures and

principles, scarcely reached through long detours and
winding curves, delights you to excess, has stolen your
attention, and allured your love to itself. How much more
then should creative Wisdom herself attract you, for
through her all these realities are fashioned that they
may exist and brought into the light that they may be
recognised? Will the winning of Wisdom not coax you to
court her much more earnestly?

Such Wisdom then is the crowning art: 'Of all the arts, this last I would
call the art, the law, the norm, the form, and the principle, the univer-
sal, uniform, invariable exemplar'. Gilbert invites Adam to become
in his turn a *doctor mellifluus,* explaining the essence and attributes
of the divine Majesty: 'On a subject of this kind willingly would I
listen to you in the chair of prophecy'. For Adam, a potential teacher
among the Cistercians, Gilbert proposes a curriculum which suggests
what he tried to convey to his monks as their teacher:

But when you had directed your attention to the divine
blessings, then willingly would I listen to you explain more
in depth and develop at greater length your views on
pardon, on grace and on glory, on what the Lord has given,
restored or added, and on all he endured for us and conferred upon us. I would listen to you review for us the
preceding sufferings in Christ and the glories to come, the
endurance of trials, the anticipation of rewards, the elements of faith, the laws of morality, the individual steps of
renewal and the stages of progress towards perfection.
Here obviously is an abundance of material and an
inviting occupation. Nowhere else can any man of talent,
however zealous and however learned, employ himself
more prolifically, more fruitfully.[53]

In his last, incomplete sermon, Gilbert comments on the teaching of the
bride, the teaching Church, in a way which reflects his own ideal of
teaching.

In all this observe the teaching of the bride, observe her
devotion, observe her loving preparation whether seeking
her Beloved or instructing her daughters or recalling his
praises. She adjures earnestly, she answers readily, she
illustrates with ornaments, she divides distinctly, she reviews briefly, she sums up concisely and I do not know
whether she expresses sufficiently. I know indeed that she
concludes affectionately: 'Such is my Beloved and he is my
friend'. Great is the compass of these praises and

obviously great is her love when she praises.[54]

Gilbert's defense of the General Chapter's prohibition against the writing of books assumes some encouragement or commission to commit his own sermons to writing:

> Great then, it must be admitted, is the value of composing the word of salvation, but only when this task is entrusted to, or better exacted of some individual. The caution, then, of our elders in imposing silence as a rule would seem to require no refutation; however extensive their caution, it does no harm, for the permission profitably granted to some might prove the occasion of rash presumption for others, while a man might engage in a task not imposed on him to the neglect of the task imposed.[55]

Because all his material seems to have passed through Gilbert's process of mastication and rumination, his sources, other than Scripture, are difficult to identify. Once he quotes St Jerome's 'Ecclesiastical Writers', and he asks a friend to obtain for him a copy of that Saint's 'Commentary on Isaiah'.[56] This request concludes the delightful letter to Brother William, otherwise unidentified, to counsel him not to unfold his ostrich wings to migrate to the court of a duke, *dux*. Since William was previously on good terms with the duke, his desire for advice may suggest that Gilbert also knew the duke and his court, and perhaps obtained manuscripts from him through William. To another friend he writes on the unexpected length of time it has taken to collate parallel passages, whether from Scripture or from commentaries, for the explanation of a text of St James.[57] In some passages, of course, one hears echoes of Roger, Aelred, and Bernard, and also of St Anselm. He is familiar with the thought behind the great prayer of St Anselm to Paul and to Christ, each as a mother.[58] Gilbert's fourth sermon Etienne Gilson considers a very personalized commentary on Anselm's 'faith seeking understanding' and an 'interesting synthesis of Augustine, Anselm and Bernard'. In a later sermon Gilbert quotes without comment the familiar text of Isaiah: 'unless you believe, you will not understand'.[59] In his fourth and fifth sermons, however, Gilbert attempts something more modest than this 'interesting synthesis'; limiting himself to an audience of believers, he tries to explain imaginatively the role of reason mediating between the starting point of faith and the goal of understanding.

In an all too brief summary of his dissertation on Gilbert, Fr Jean Vuong-Dinh-Lam writes:

> The sources of Gilbert are above all St Augustine whom he uses in his theology of original sin, grace, liberty and

predestination. The Rule of St Benedict is his guide in his
teaching of monastic observance. He seems to have read
John Cassian. St Gregory the Great is very familiar to him.
But in his spiritual teaching his undisputed master is
St Bernard, whom of course he never plagiarizes.

Yet Fr Jean also notes minor differences and omissions. For the image
of the Trinity in Man, Gilbert chooses not the augustinian 'memory,
intellect, and will', but the pauline 'flesh, soul, and spirit'. Again,
though man is estranged from himself and becomes like a striped, not a
spotted leopard, *dissimilis sibi,* and though he inhabits other mountains
than Sion, Fr Jean observes that Gilbert avoids the expression
regio dissimilitudinis.[60]

RELIGIOUS EXPERIENCE

A reading of Gilbert is more rewarding if one pauses to chew and savor
his words. Gilbert is an experience. He has found the Beloved. Here we
must note that Etienne Gilson, indulging perhaps a penchant for paradox but as quotable as ever, concludes some remarks on Gilbert by
saying: 'Gilbert was not a great mystic, perhaps no mystic at all, and in
his commentary he prudently remains on the level of the "moral
interpretation". But he has a strong and well-poised mind, and his
writings are well worth reading'. This remark about an author whom
members of his Order considered a theologian and specifically a
mystical theologian, is devastating praise, as if one should say of a poet
that he writes well but has no inspiration. After pondering over Gilbert's
writings for many years, Edmond Mikkers protests that Gilson's remark
is too harsh, indeed that 'from a greater familiarity with Gilbert's
sermons, it is evident that he had reached a high level of prayer, not to
say an intimate union with God'. Fr Mikkers considers that Gilbert
was most dedicated to contemplation of heavenly mysteries, 'unless we
wish to suppose that he has almost nowhere spoken from his own
experience, when he proposes for us his most bountiful teaching on
contemplation'. Mystical experience would seem necessary to explain
his writings. Not without reason then should we emphasize for further
study the ten characteristics of his religious experience which Fr Pierre
Miquel carefully documents:[61]

1. experience is a principal source of his teaching;
2. personal experience must be tested against the touch-
    stone of Scripture and the communal experience of

the Church;
3. spiritual experience differs from experience of the senses;
4. experience is a foretaste of what faith undertakes to believe;
5. experience allows the soul to perceive what it cannot understand;
6. experience is a gift the soul can prepare itself to receive;
7. experience of the word of God varies with the disposition of those to whom it is addressed;
8. experience is incommunicable and its memory difficult to recall;
9. experience, however brief, compensates for many labors;
10. experience is full of joy.

Fr Miquel concludes with a quotation from Sermon eight, which he says is full of delightful theology and throbbing with the clarity of experience.[62] Gilbert asks how we can bridge the gap between our natures, vain and void, and the union of two natures in the one person of Christ, the mystery he has been teaching. His conclusion is his ever-present theme of love:

> Is it perhaps that charity is winged and soars over this intervening gulf of which we are speaking, with the swift flight of ardent desire? Yes, I agree. For to love is already to possess; to love is also to be assimilated and united. But why not, since God is charity?

The great gulf between our nature and the nature of God cannot be bridged except by faith and especially by charity. Etienne Gilson and M.-André Fracheboud have noted in Gilbert's first eight sermons that he clearly lays down the distinctions which would lay the ghost of the charge of pantheism levelled against Gilbert as against Bernard. Though Gilbert does not use the word *deificatio*, he has laid the foundation for the development of his teaching on divinisation.[63]

THE NORTH WIND

To idealize the life at Swineshead as a happy blend of cult, culture, and agriculture, a romantic era of sweetness and light, an idyllic and pastoral retirement, is to pass over some harsh realities, the shades of darkness and bitter night which Gilbert pictures. He warns his monks about questionable quests for Jesus and his holy name:

> He is made the subject of a treatise in councils, of a debate
> in courts, of a dispute in the schools, of a song in churches.
> These preoccupations are religious; but go to the harbor
> mouth and consider the result of this stream of activity. See
> if all this is not a kind of haggling over the price of Christ.
> It is a lucrative business, the name of Christ. Nothing is
> more prized, nothing more desirable. Happy none the less
> is he who prizes the excellence of this name. Among
> others let there be treatises, lawsuits, disputations about
> this name. For us it is enough if, in our cloisters at least,
> this name be loved.[64]

The locks of his bride were torn by almost continuous schisms in the
Church throughout Gilbert's lifetime. He refers to the rift in her ranks
under Pope Innocent II (1130–43) when Cardinal Peter of the
Pierleoni family was 'elected' with the name of Anacletus II,
antipope (1130–1138). The Roman Emperor here was Lothaire II
(1125–37) and the Lion, Cardinal Pierleoni.

> But the flocks do not listen to nor rejoice at the voice of
> the Bridegroom but rather at the voice of the Roman
> Emperor. Unless (and this we have more reason to admit)
> they do not so much rejoice as tremble at his roar. There-
> fore they cannot be moved at the roaring of the Lion,
> because they are held fast by the immovable seal of divine
> knowledge.[65]

Later in this sermon, Gilbert laments the dispersal of bishops and the
impoverishment of clerics and monks. He speaks bluntly about the
weakness of Alexander III (1159–1181) who was opposed by the
antipope, Victor IV (1159–64), with the support of Emperor Frederick
Barbarossa (1152–90). Victor was the first of a line of antipopes who
relied on friends and supporters of Barbarossa.

> Recall Lord Jesus, your children who are astray, to the
> sweetness of this milk [of the bride], that from the mouths
> of sucklings you may elicit praise when you have destroyed
> the foe and the victor. Hasten then and exchange judge-
> ment for victory, in order that those who call upon your
> name may dwell in unity, because in this unity you send
> blessings and life.[66]

In changing times, he knows the abbot's duty to protect his monks:

> He must appear in court, attend councils, coax rulers,
> thwart rustlers, refute prosecutors, pay judges' fees, recon-
> cile with the world those whose conversation, like Paul's,

has been in heaven. There were times when we used to drink the milk of the nations and be nourished at the breasts of kings; and see, now they importunately demand a recompense for what we imbibed perhaps a little too freely. But while nations and kings squeeze barren breasts too violently, they draw blood with the milk of their temporal subjects, not this blood of the flesh but blood of the soul . . . . That blood . . . they siphon and drink, causing excessive anguish. Alas how our world is turned upside down.[67]

Gilbert cautions against imitating those in office whose example is less than edifying: 'Why emulate whose who, appointed to offices, are compared to beasts of burden? Their eyes stare at the earth, their maws crop the earth. With zest they ruminate on it, they devour it with relish and though they have lofty positions they wallow in the mire'.[68] He does not refrain from criticizing men of his own Order for ambition and presumption; perhaps in an era of decline, which Fr Mikkers suggests may have prompted both Gilbert and Roger of Byland to consider resignation, these new problems may have arisen from the conflict between Henry II and Thomas à Becket:[69]

Our age, fallen into decline, has introduced other ways. We must now provide abundance for permanent residents and delicacies for transients. Nor by transients do I mean lay folk, for why should I pass judgement on outsiders? Among them however, the usual moderation may not be observed, for they can scarcely tolerate rationing where they imagine the existence of supplies of all kinds. But why should I advert to those whose god is their belly? Why the very ones who profess and preach abstinence, the very primates of the Order, how finicky they are in the houses of others! What an eye they have for banquets of rare foods prepared for a gourmet! How they wrinkle their foreheads, turn up their noses and look askance, if anything is served with less taste and less festivity![70]

The monastery of Swineshead endured such hard times, probably in the winter of 1165-66, that the monks lacked even their daily bread. As reasons Gilbert gives not only crop failure but also calumnies and mockery from worldlings and problems with neighboring or other lords. So great was their destitution that Gilbert must share his deep grief with his monks:

How long, O Lord, will the north wind of adversity oppress our regions? . . . Often must I groan and my heart

grieve. Children beg for bread and there is no one to break
it for them, for there is none to be broken. I do not speak
of the bread of the Word but of this daily food for the
body. Yet my soul cannot be filled with the richness of
that heavenly bread, as long as lack of this daily bread
causes, as it were, the emaciation of grief. Distracted by the
sound of this lament, I have forgotten to eat that heavenly
bread. A harsh north wind is exterior hardship but much
harsher is anxiety of mind. One of the two weighs on you,
brethren; both together oppress me. I carry a burden among
you because of our common distress and a distress of my
own beyond yours, because it is on your behalf. Hence
cases of misfortune, hence legal quarrels arise. Some
whisper, others taunt, and what is beyond human effort to
prevent from happening, they turn into a reproach when it
happens. Some provoke, some mock, attributing bad luck
to folly.[71]

Yet if Gilbert, like Roger of Byland, desired to resign, to exchange
the mantle of an abbot for the mantle of pure contemplation (his
desire could well have been a sigh for heaven) his actual resignation
lacks contemporary evidence. Fr Mikkers, an authority on chronicles,
sees in the words of the Chronicler, 'formerly abbot of Hoiland in
England', a possible suggestion of Gilbert's resignation. Though Gilbert
often inveighs against ambition and warns Roger against ambition and
presumption, he advises Roger not to resign. Gilbert's deprecatory
remarks about himself in that context show only his own real feelings
of unworthiness. Roger, if consulted, would have been likely to dissuade
Gilbert from resignation and his continuing reputation suggests that no
reason existed to remove him from office. The simplest explanation is
the final suggestion of Fr Mikkers that on his journey to or from a
General Chapter, whether his intention had been to seek acceptance of
his resignation there or not, Gilbert stopped at L'Arrivour and was
overtaken by death. He has merited a place in menologies, a feast day
on May 25th, and he is listed by many authors as Blessed Gilbert.[72]

Gilbert deserves his share in the eulogies given to that constellation
of Cistercian writers who arose in the twelfth century. Let what has
been said be applied to him. His exuberant and sparkling style is not
explained by suggesting that before or after entering a monastery he
frequented a classical school. His Latin shows a wealth of experience,
a brilliance which recalls the colors of autumn. He manifests a flexibility,
a liveliness, and a poetic precision, which will surprise every new

reader today. Like his fellow Cistercian writers, he found a way to sanctity even while 'succumbing', in an honored Christian tradition, 'to the greatest temptation, which was to become a man of letters'.[73]

The luminous statement of the medieval Chronicler with which we began and the brilliant modern paradoxes with which we are tempted to end require refinement. The early Cistercians engaged in a life and death struggle against distortion of the Christian message in an era not only of war and schism, not only of powerful and longlived potentates, but also of an emerging scholasticism which they held suspect. In the midst of renewal, upheaval, and revolution, inside and outside the Church, they were dedicated to an integral Christianity taught in the school of Christ, part of which was their literary style. 'Dom Gilbert', according to the Chronicler, 'composed the sermons . . . following with great distinction and learning the manner and style of Blessed Bernard'. Gilson has written briefly and brilliantly on Bernard's highly personal Latin style, and in a memorable essay Christine Mohrmann examines Bernard's vocabulary, syntax, and style.[74] In Bernard's corpus, which required secretaries and included much business correspondence, many 'exotic words' have been compiled;[75] in Gilbert no word occurs without precedent in classical or early ecclesiastical Latin. Structuralists could more easily analyze Gilbert's sermons individually and in groups than Bernard's. Bernard ranges freely and needs no apology for wandering from his text; rarely, and always with an apology, does Gilbert stray from the text being discussed, for he is ever conscious of the unity and pattern of his work. Bernard's sermons share his ubiquity and his ambassadorship to all Europe; Gilbert seems more conscious of adaptation to the needs of the little people who listen to him and whose work he shared in the environment of the fens. Traditions robbed neither author of his individuality.

Miss Mohrmann's remarks about Bernard's syntax apply equally to Gilbert, namely that parallel clauses (*parataxis*) are more dominant than subordinate clauses (*hypotaxis*), that the laws of structure are simple and normal and reflect the practice of fourth and fifth century prose. She notes that Bernard's literary figures, antithesis, parallelism, rhyme, assonance, and alliteration, suffice to mark the structure of phrases and the course of thought. Miss Mohrmann's statements seem as true of Gilbert and her examples from Bernard could be paralleled in Gilbert. Applicable to both authors also are her remarks about the play on the sound and significance of words, on images and metaphors. The works of both authors are like mosaics sparkling with untranslatable tesserae.

Let Gilbert's remarks about Bernard with which we began serve as our first examples of style. Gilbert shies away from repeating Bernard's remarks about the kinds of anointing, and substitutes an explanation of the various ways of anointing; he uses a mnemonic with anaphora, parataxis, and rhyme, to help recall his four points: 'some people are touched, and others sprinkled, some are daubed and others drenched / *alii tanguntur, alii asperguntur, alii inunguntur, alii perfunduntur*'.[76] Again he says that Bernard interpreted the bride's beauty with a master's touch, and with alliteration, rhyme, hypotaxis, and humor, refuses to comment on Bernard: 'Whether the master be the more remarkable for learning or for eloquence I know not, but the matter in the pages of his homilies it ill becomes me to turn over for discussion, pardon me, with my little finger / *Et quae vir (utrum eruditior an eloquentior nescio) suis disputavit in homiliis, nec minimo (ut sic dicam) digito, decuit a nobis ad discutiendum attingi*'.[77] Here are a teacher's paratactical *sententiae*: 'a good conscience is bold for its charity is not cold; it lives without fright, for love sets it alight; it does not blush before the Beloved, for love trusts the Beloved / *Bona conscientia audet, et charitas ardet. Illa non formidat, ista inflammat. Illa pro dilecto non confunditur, ista inflammat.* And again: 'preoccupation entangles, repose unravels the spirit / *animum cura implicat, quies explicat*',[78] and speaking of the bride:

> Because the bride seeks him by night, in my opinion, her quest is less for the sight of him than for his embrace. She desires to hold him rather than to behold him. Seeing is good indeed but seizing unites more closely / *Quae per noctes quaerit, non videtur mihi tam aspectus quam amplexus sectari. Tenere magis optat quam intueri. Bona quidem visio est, sed adhaesio arctior.*

Here finally is a line made intentionally memorable by alliteration: 'if you will pardon the rhyme, faith enfolds, reason upholds, understanding beholds / *et (ut sic dicam) fides tenet, tuetur ratio, intelligentia intuetur*'.[79]

Gilson concludes his comments on the literary character of the style of the first Cistercians and particularly of St Bernard:

> They fled from the world, but the strongest temptation that assailed the most detached amongst them all had been to become a man of letters; and he found ways to become a saint even when he succumbed. In spite of his formidable asceticism St Bernard was no puritan when it came to literature. The walls of his monasteries were bare, but his style was not bare . . . ; each and all of these hardy ascetics carried in his bosom a humanist who by no

means wanted to die.[80]

Miss Mohrmann introduces her essay with a re-examination of these stark paradoxes. She finds here a dichotomy, a tension of opposite poles, as if, despite all their detachment, the early Cistercians failed to become detached from a humanist tradition not only because they used the classics and citations from profane authors but also because they valued careful writing and an ornate style. They were equally guilty, but guilty of what?

To understand what Bernard opposed, especially at the prompting of William of St Thierry, is to appreciate what Bernard proposed and practised, abetted by Aelred and Gilbert in their own regions. The contemporary school of Chartres, notes Miss Mohrmann, leaned towards speculative and scientific thought, while Abelard was showing his predilection for dialectic. With peculiar insight the Cistercians opposed what was a new *quaestio*, a dialectic which was also a literary form, and an 'aristotelianism' which came to be adopted as an orderly and structured foundation for scholastic thought. Not that questions and sentences and structured explanations were such novelties in the history of thought or in the history of the Church.[81] Suddenly one hears a Gilbert clearly stating that the business of the monk is the quest, not the question. His statement was more than literary gymnastics; it was a memorable phrase which signified a deep division between an ancient and integral Christian and monastic humanism and a structural theology which taught in a new style and sought out and integrated pure theological ideas.[82] This newly developing approach to theology seemed to limit Scripture to its literal and historical sense, to subordinate Scripture in majors and minors to theological conclusions, to warm the mind of man but to leave his heart cold, to feed the philosopher and let the poet go hungry. Gilson called the Cistercian opposition an anti-philosophism and singled out Gilbert as its greatest proponent, as if indeed Bernard, Gilbert, and the Cistercians were anti-intellectuals.[83] What would be singularly present in Aquinas at the peak of scholasticism, the Cistercians thought singularly absent in its beginnings, the acknowledgement that much learning, love, and life was available at the foot of the Cross.

Let us return to the paradox of the Cistercians' bare walls and ornate style. Was their return to primitive Christianity and to a 'rusticity' of life flagrantly contradicted by their brilliant literary style? Let us concede with Miss Mohrmann that Bernard's style is neither simple nor bare but lively, spirited, and emotionally gripping, at times perhaps flowery and, in Miss Mohrmann's word, 'baroque'. Let us agree with her and with Jean Leclercq that these monks, before or after their

entry into cloister, received a classical training which was preparatory
to the study of wisdom and which left its mark on their genius and
writings. Yet such training does not fully explain their taste for good
speaking and writing, or account for their particular literary style.
Miss Mohrmann examines Gilson's joyful paradox which may suggest
that their literary training was in *impedimentum,* worldly baggage
which deserved to be jettisoned. Their style, far from rustic, according
to Miss Mohrmann, was part of their return to primitive monasticism,
to an integral Christianity, to the school of Christ and the examples of
the apostles. Miss Mohrmann finds this style in the ancient Latin
translation of the first letter of St Clement of Rome, in Tertullian, in
St Cyprian, and especially in the Confessions of St Augustine.

As in doctrine the early Cistercians looked to the original school of
Christ and to primitive monasticism, so in their spoken and written
word they were responsible for a renascence of a paleo-christian style
which had reached a peak in the fourth and fifth centuries. Without
relinquishing their own individualities, Bernard and Gilbert shared that
renascence. But one can not underestimate the influence of the Vulgate
and of the Fathers who commented on its books precisely in the
stylistic characteristics Miss Mohrmann singles out. What was the
source of their co-ordination rather than subordination of clauses
(parataxis rather than *hypotaxis,* proceeding by *kola* and *kommata)*
if not their daily recital and hourly rumination on the psalms? What
more paratactical than the Beatitudes? What more figurative than the
Canticle or the parables of the Lord? What greater play on words than
on the names of Peter and Paul? What more paradoxical than the
statement that 'he who loses his life, will save it'? What better known
or more filled with rhetorical figures than St Paul's letter on charity?
This is an important point, but it does not destroy Miss Mohrmann's
nuanced and brilliant essay which traces also the influence of the large
body of homiletic and mystical literature. Of course Miss Mohrmann
knows that the Lord had style. Renewed interest in the twelfth
century has focused attention on the spiritual aliveness of the
Cistercians whom contemporaries faulted for their primitive and rustic
monasticism and their revival of a scriptural and paleochristian literary
style. Their school studied the integral Christ and their word embraced
all the senses of Scripture. Bernard was the last Father of the Church
and also deserved his title *doctor mellifluus.* With him Cistercians were
in the mainstream of spiritual and mystical theology and living
participants in the paleochristian renascence of literary style.

SERMONS ON THE CANTICLE

The many commentaries on the Canticle in the twelfth century indicate a renascence of interest in the allegory of divine love comparable to the renascence of interest in Ovid and amatory literature. The Canticle provided a terminology, a continuing imaginative support, a pedagogical tool in presenting ascetical and mystical theology for those who by profession were lovers of God. Neither Bernard nor Gilbert was daunted by prudery in discussing the physical features mentioned in the Canticle, but with realism and discretion avoided what Eric Colledge calls 'the simple but not always wise fervours of *Brautmystik*', popular in that century 'especially among women religious'. Like Bernard, Gilbert adapted the Canticle of human love to the union of the individual soul with God, of the monastic city with its Lord, and of the Church with Christ. His sermons, not pulpit oratory but chats in the Horatian manner, use many a lively apostrophe and much dramatic dialogue, each sermon being polished for publication as *litterarius sermo*. Each has its own unity, like a letter of Seneca or of Pliny, and can be summed up in a chapter-heading or in a topic sentence with the bride or the lover as subject.[84]

Verses 3:1–4 of the Canticle are treated by Bernard in his last twelve sermons (SC 75–86) and by Gilbert in his first thirteen. Gilbert does not establish a link between his own and Bernard's sermons, as John of Ford would do later in the prologue of his sermons on the Canticle, where he indicates his debt to Bernard and Gilbert, whose work he continued and completed. Gilbert establishes a link between the end of the second and the beginning of the third chapter of the Canticle, between the bride's consolation during the tryst in the spring when the Beloved is present and her desolation when her Beloved seems absent. His mastery of his medium suggests that already with encouragement from others he had been composing oral or written sermons on the first two chapters of the Canticle; nor should it surprise anyone if a Jean Leclercq were to discover and identify Gilbert's sermons on the first two chapters of the Canticle.

Gilbert's first words indicate his emphasis on the affections of lovers, *affectus amatium,* an expression to be found in an epistle of *Seneca noster*. His sermons can be divided into groups, of which the first three are easily established, as they follow the divisions of the Canticle itself. The first group of eight sermons Gilbert summarizes in the last paragraph of the eighth sermon: the bride seeks and finds; her quest for her Beloved ends in discovery. The central emphasis is on the *circuitus,* a spiritual pilgrimage for the proficient in search of the Beloved in the planned city of God, and the climax is in the eighth sermon on charity, the union with the Beloved. The ever gentle Henri de Lubac comments a little impishly on the *circuitus:* 'at least that day, Gilbert inherited the inspiration of Bernard'. The first paragraph of the fifth sermon is an engaging explanation of what the Cistercians meant by rumination on the sacred word.[85]

In the second group of sermons (9–14), Gilbert addresses one individual, the privileged lover who has reached a more perfect union with the Beloved. Of these five sermons (eleven and twelve are parts of the same sermon) the first four develop a half-verse of the bride, Sg 3:4: 'I have taken hold of him and I will not let him go, until I bring him into my mother's house and into the chamber of the one who conceived me'. Sermon fourteen, the last and richest, still dwells on the transport of union but in the words of the Bridegroom, Sg 3:5: 'I adjure you, daughters of Jerusalem, by the gazelles and the hinds of the fields, that you do not arouse or awaken the beloved until she herself pleases'. This verse, a refrain already sung in Sg 2:7, and previously discussed by Bernard (SC 52), would recur in Sg 8:4, to be treated later by John of Ford in his Sermons 98–99. Gilbert addresses the individual possessed of some extraordinary habit of virtue: 'Of the man clad in such a habit of virtue that for him virtue seems to have become second nature, I would say that he has not so much embraced as been embraced by virtue'.[86] Since nature is fickle, such a soul needs continued attention and diligence to retain the Beloved in the memory, to contemplate him, to exchange contemplation for works of charity out of persevering love for him. The sleep of such a soul in the lair of mystery should not be disturbed until the Spirit awakens it.

The third group of sermons (S 15–21) is addressed to nuns, literally, it seems, rather than as a literary figure. The sermons explain a chorus of the Canticle assigned to the daughters of Jerusalem (Sg 3:6–11) and form a unity of their own. These felicitous sermons, though applicable to all, Gilbert happily addresses to nuns who were affecting a Cistercian way of life. Here Gilbert teaches with rich colors and emotion adapted to the individual souls in a widening circle, a chorus of lovers progressing along the Cistercian way. His literary and spiritual art solved a practical problem in a way any feminine reader would appreciate. The nuns were hungry sheep looking up to be fed. Gilbert remembered them in this group of sermons where the center of unity is the deceptively simple and hauntingly beautiful sermon nineteen, a pivotal sermon on charity.[87]

The lengthy address of the Bridegroom, Sg 4:1–15, is discussed by Gilbert in sixteen sermons (S 22–37). Here Gilbert writes some of his most brilliant passages, of which the most symbolic is his comparison of the Cistercians to a pomegranate, the seeds united in spirit within the rind of the cloister. Since Gilbert does not subdivide this longer group, the following summary may be pardoned:

S 22. The lover has the pure and simple eye of a dove,

S 23. ascends to His wisdom and discerns what is good,

S 24. begets twins, the light of understanding and the warmth of affection.

S 25. Modestly the lover has no clear vision of personal progress,

S 26. guarded by battlements of the word and of charity,

S 27. and feasts on spiritual food to give milk to babes.

S 28. Purified, the lover's prayer rises like incense.

S 29. The lover is invited from Lebanon to a crown,

S 30. and longs for union of minds and hearts.

S 31. The lover offers material and spiritual milk to babes,

S 32. is fragrant with the ointments of the Anointed,

S 33. and is anointed with spirit, power, mercy and all graces.

S 34. The lover pleases in works, lips and spirit,

S 35. offers rich fruit from the fountain in the garden,

S 36. produces spices of all the virtues,

S 37. and is a well and a fountain, wise and loving.

The final eleven sermons (S 38–48) form smaller groups to match the dialogue in the Canticle. The first three develop the response of the bride to the Bridegroom:

S 38. The lover is affected by north and south winds,

S 39. but distinguishes freedom, affectivity and grace,

S 40. and bears fruits of continence, repentence, and all virtues.

Gilbert then devotes one sermon to the invitation of the Bridegroom:

S 41. The lover is invited to a banquet with milk, honey and wine.

In the next five sermons, Gilbert develops the words of the bride, Sg 5:2–8:

S 42. The lover welcomes His visit and visits those who are His,

S 43. is led to contemplation by His inspiration to action,

S 44. but opens the cloistered door only to find him gone.

S 45. Advised by watchmen, the lover dons or discards the mantle of office;

S 46. the lover languishes with love.

In his last two sermons Gilbert examines the desire of the chorus to see the Bridegroom and introduces the bride's description of him:

S 47.   The lover teaches others the beauty of the Nazarite,

S 48.   and shows him radiant with light and red with fire.

Thus apparently Gilbert had availed himself of permission to comment on the Canticle. He understood and followed the divisions of its dialogue and its chorus, the pastoral song of Shepherd and shepherdess, the epithalamium of the bride and her Bridegroom. Sedulous to avoid the repetition of Bernard, yet following Bernard's manner and style, he showed his own mastery of the art of the literary sermon. He had done his own work of masticating the sacred word, benefitted from his own experience, and passed on the fruit with his own hand. As with Bernard, so with Gilbert, the work was cut short all too soon, but not left unfinished, thanks to the later labor of John of Ford.[88]

THE SEVEN TREATISES

Three treatises have already been mentioned: the first and seventh addressed to Roger of Byland, and the fifth, a reply to a friend unknown to us, on the meaning of a verse in St James. Of the four remaining treatises, the second and third are addressed to his brethren, the fourth and sixth each to a friend unnamed. The first four treatises and the sixth brilliantly and imaginatively illumine Gilbert's spiritual theology and are complementary to his sermons: the first explores the contemplation of heaven; the second compares the quest of the Beloved 'here' with the vision of him 'there', according to measure; the third compares the joy on the way with the rejoicing in the fatherland; the fourth shows how conversation and colloquy are but the shadows of substance; and the sixth presents a moving picture of the flow of redemptive grace. The first part of the long seventh treatise vigorously attacks ambition and presumption, while the second half considers the burdens of the office of abbot and Roger's excellent qualifications for remaining in office.

GILBERT'S ONE INCOMPLETE SERMON AND FOUR EPISTLES

Gilbert has left us one incomplete sermon on the word of God as a seed, in which with good humor at his own expense, he admits his use and abuse of a scriptural text. His first and fourth epistles seem to concern abbot Richard of Fountains, the third of that name (1150–70); in the fourth, while deferring a definitive answer to a friend unknown, Gilbert adverts to the abbot of Fountains as overshadowing him again with a great cloud of witnesses; in the first, addressed to a Brother R. not further identified, he may be uneasily accepting an offer of reconciliation from the same abbot, Richard of Fountains, who apparently had sent him a peace offering of a crozier, a woolen vestment, and two chalices. Gilbert's second epistle, his vocation letter to Adam, pictures a scholarly cleric with a large following of pupils; the tenor of this letter seems to contradict Gilson's comment that Gilbert was the one among the Cistercians who most fully developed Bernard's anti-philosophism. Gilbert shows that he is not confused about his priorities; Aristotle, Seneca, and other authors are clearly presented as propaedeutic to the study of wisdom. Adam is invited to seize the opportunity to advance in monastic theology when Gilbert outlines with some completeness what might be called a monastic curriculum. Gilbert's third epistle, as we have seen, with humor and satire warns Brother William, otherwise unidentified, about advancing to the court of a duke, also unidentified.

Almost incidentally, concluding the fourth treatise with a passage about the disciples and the Lord on the way to Emmaus, Gilbert allows an insight into his idea of a letter, a treatise, or a sermon: 'Well at least we have chatted a little with you, O Lord, and about you'. Frequently he invokes the Lord and writes fervent passages which may easily be turned into moving prayers punctuated by his favorite apostrophe: *O bone Jesu* and *O dulcis Jesu*. Knowing how evanescent is even the written word, Gilbert recalls how Jesus wrote in the sand words to be scattered by the wind and foresees the disappearance of his *literarius sermo* with the end of our time: 'When the eternal day dawns, the lamp of prophetic teaching will flicker out and the flood of written speech will ebb away.'[89]

MANUSCRIPTS, EDITIONS AND A TRANSLATION

Fr Mikkers lists and locates forty-eight complete or partial manuscripts of Gilbert on the Canticle, but few for his other works. He also examines the many doubtful or spurious works, among which those preserved in an unedited manuscript in the Bodleian Library and written in England about the year 1200, deserve further investigation and independent evidence.[90] Fr Mikkers considers reliable the text of the Mabillon edition (1690) and thinks variant readings from the collation of manuscripts show only accidental differences. He considers the text of the Florentine editions unreliable, however, because of faulty readings of the manuscripts. The various reprints of Mabillon by Migne exhibit misprints which vary with successive reprintings. The Latin text in *Oeuvres Complètes de Saint Bernard,* accompanying the French translation by P. Dion, repeats some misprints from Migne and adds a few of its own.

For this English translation I have relied on Fr Mikkers' evaluation of Mabillon's text. Textual problems are indicated in footnotes to the translation. No translation can hope to match the prose-poetry of a work on the Canticle written 'after the manner and style of Blessed Bernard'. Readers will recognize that 'the best of translations can express, not the exact meaning of the original, but the closest approximation possible in another tongue'.[91] Prudent librarians will continue to find space for Mabillon and Migne, those extraordinary giants of industry on whose shoulders we climb. Roger of Byland's vocation letter, *Lac parvulorum,* was delightfully introduced and edited by C. H. Talbot who had the benefit of notes made by the late André Wilmart, a scholar to whom all Cistercian students are much indebted.[89] We do need, however, a companion volume to this translation, written with an insight and love to match that with which Amédée Hallier presented the writings and life of St Aelred.[90]

To assist in the preparation of these volumes, I was given financial assistance from the Research Board of the University of Manitoba, and the firm and enthusiastic assistance of the board of editors of Cistercian Publications. Any inadequacies in the work are mine.

[Cistercian Publications regrets that technical difficulties have prevented the use of accents in the notes to this volume—ed.]

NOTES TO INTRODUCTION

1. Etienne Gilson, *The Mystical Theology of Saint Bernard* tr. A. H. C. Downes (London: Sheed and Ward, 1940) 2-6; Jean Leclercq, *The Love of Learning and the Desire for God: a study of monastic culture,* tr. Catharine Misrahi (N.Y.: Fordham Press, 1961).

2. J. Leclercq, C. H. Talbot, H. M. Rochais, *S. Bernardi Opera* (Rome: Editiones cistercienses, 1957-58) vv. 1-2; Edmund Mikkers, Hilary Costello, *Joannis de Ford: super extremam partem Cantici Canticorum sermones CXX;* CC Continuatio Mediaevalis 17, 18 (Turnholt: Brepols, 1970) vv. 1-2; Joannes Mabillon, *Sancti Bernardi Opera Omnia* (1690, rpt. Milan: Gnocchi, 1850-52) 3:1-302, Migne, PL 183 (Paris: 1854) 1-298 (hereafter Mab. and Migne).

3. Edmond Mikkers, 'De Vita et Operibus Gilberti de Hoylandia', *Citeaux* 14 (1963) 33-43, 265-279; M. Jean Vuong-dinh-Lam, 'Doctrine spiri-tuelle de Gilbert de Hoyland d'apres son commentaire sur le Cantique' (unpublished dissertation for the Faculty of the Anselmianum, vv. 1-2, Rome, 1963); 'Le Monastere: foyer de vie spirituelle d'apres Gilbert de Hoyland', Coll. 26 (1964) 5-21; 'Les Observances Monastiques: instruments de vie spiri-tuelle d'apres Gilbert de Hoyland', Coll. 26 (1964) 169-199; 'Gilbert de Hoy-land', DSp (1967) 371-4; Pierre Miquel, 'Les Caracteres de l'Experience Religieuse d'apres Gilbert de Hoyland', Coll. 27 (1965) 150-59 (hereafter Lam, Mikkers and Miquel).

4. Mikkers cites Cave, Lelong, Hardy, de Visch, the *Acta Sanctorum* and *Dictionary of National Biography* for the claim that Gilbert was a monk at Clairvaux; one may add David Knowles, C. N. L. Brooke and Vera C. M. London, *The Heads of Religious Houses in England and Wales, 940-1216* (Cambridge U. Press, 1972) 144, relying on C. Henriques, *Menologium Cister-ciense* (Antwerp, 1630) 172. Ailbe J. Luddy claims Gilbert for Scotland and Pastoret for Ireland, according to Mikkers, but he is claimed for England by H. Reiklinger's *Lexikon,* by DNB and by C. J. Holdsworth, in 'John of Ford and English Cistercian Writing', *Transactions of the Royal Historical Society* 5th ser. 11 (1961) 122; the new edition of John of Ford by Edmund Mikkers and Hilary Costello, I:viii, calls him *abbas quidam anglicanus.*

5. Mikkers 34, gives the history and vouches for the fidelity of this state-ment to the original text of the larger Chronicle of Clairvaux now lost: *'Hic reverendus, egregius atque devotissimus et doctissimus pater dominus Gislebertus, quondam abbas de Hoylandia in Anglia, fecit et composuit sermones in hoc volumine contentos super Cantica Canticorum valde notabiliter et scientifices in sequendo modum et stilum beati Bernardi. Et apud monasterium de Rippatorio obiit anno Domini MCLXXII.'*

6. Compare S 22:1, with Bernard SC 40:4 and 45:1-3; S 33:6, with Bernard SC 10ff; S 20:1, with Bernard Ep 2:2; SBOp 4:302.

7.   Knowles, *Heads,* 140.

8.   Amedee Hallier, *The Monastic Theology of Aelred of Rievaulx* (CS 2, Spencer, Mass. 1969) xxi, n. 9, David Knowles' introduction, p. x.

9.   Mikkers, 36-7.

10.   *Walter Daniel's Life of Ailred,* ed. and trans. F. M. Powicke (London: Nelson, 1950) xxxix.

11.   S 41:4.

12.   Henri de Lubac, *Exegese Medieval* (Paris: Aubier, 1959-64) 1:602-3, n. 1.

13.   S 41:7-9, Aelred, *Spiritual Friendship* (CF5, 1974).

14.   Knowles, *Heads,* 133-4 and 129; also C. H. Talbot, 'A Letter of Roger, Abbot of Byland', ASOC 7 (1951) 219-21.

15.   Talbot, 220 and n. 4; 222 and n. 2.

16.   For the Congregation of Savigny and its impact on the Cistercian Order, see Bennet D. Hill, *English Cistercian Monasteries and their patrons in the twelfth century* (Urbana: U. of Illinois Press, 1968) 80-115, especially 98-107; see also Jacqueline Buhot, 'L'Abbaye Normande de Savigny', *Moyen Age* 46 (1936) 1-19, 104-121, 178-190, 249-272.

17.   Mikkers, 36-7.

18.   David Knowles, J. K. D. St Joseph, *Monastic Sites from the Air* (Cambridge U. Press, 1952) 90.

19.   Talbot, 221 and n. 4; G. makes the same points, T7^2:7-11.

20.   Mikkers, 37 nn. 31, 32.

21.   Talbot, 219; Mikkers, 273 n. 93. 'The laws which governed the *modus epistolaris* were observed in the composition of the most ordinary letters', Leclercq, *Love of Learning,* 223 and 369 nn. 112-4; Leclercq notes Roger's letter in 'Le genre epistolaire au moyen age', *Revue du moyen age latin* 2 (1955) 170 n. 5.

22.   For Cis as Harsh, see T 7^1:5; similar etymologies are frequent in Gilbert. 'St. Jerome, followed by Isidore and numerous other compilers, had explained the etymology of place names and of the names of persons', Leclercq, *Love of Learning,* 96.

23.   See Ep 2.

24.   Talbot, 221-2.

25.   VCH, *Lincolnshire,* 145 and n. 10, 146 and n. 2.

26.   See H. E. Hallam, *Settlement and Society,* (Cambridge U. Press, 1965) 58.

27.   VCH, *Lincolnshire,* 145 and n. 10; for the benefactions of William of Roumara, earl of Lincoln, see Hill, *English Cistercian Monasteries,* 35-6; for later grants see Hallam, *Settlement and Society,* 58-9, 41 n. 2. 69, 147, 151, 156.

28.   Jacqueline Buhot, 'L'Abbaye Normande de Savigny', 184.

29.   Knowles, *Monastic Sites,* 78; for Swineshead, at p. 278, photographs ET 58-60, this volume notes three air photographs in the Catalogue of Air Photographs of Religious Houses in the Cambridge University Collection.

30.   Hallam, *Settlement and Society,* 220-1 and *passim.*

31.   See S 6:1, S 45:6, and index under *abbot, prelate, preacher, teacher, Cistercian.*

32.   Plurals of address are used throughout the one sermon not on the Canticle, and in S 30, S 41, T 2 and T 3.

33.   De Lubac, *Exegese,* 2:586, comments on S 30:5 and numerous other passages, that the Church and the soul are inseparable in Gilbert as in Bernard. Gilbert, who often directs his remarks to the individual in the community, is cited by Cornelius a Lapide, *Commentaria in Scripturam Sacram* (re-ed, Augustine Crampon, Paris: Vives, 1860) 7:603, 608; 8:69, 71, 72, 76, 79, 80, 116, 117, 118. In the first note to each sermon below, the audience is indicated; see also 'Nuns in the Audience of Gilbert of Hoyland', in SMC 11 (1976).

34.   See S 16:4-5 and S 16:8.

35. Probably on the strength of this passage, S 40:2-3, Mikkers suggested that this sermon may have been given to nuns, but see 'Nuns in Gilbert'. Aelred of Rievaulx relates the story of the nun of Watton, reprinted in PL 195:789-95. See also Powicke, *Life of Ailred,* lxxxi-lxxxii, and Aelred Squire, *Aelred of Rievaulx* (London: SPCK, 1969) 117-8. Some authors misread Gilbert of Hoyland for Gilbert of Sempringham in Aelred's account of the nun of Watton and the nun with visions.

36. Mikkers, 39-40.

37. For Gilbert of Sempringham see Raymonde Foreville in DSp 6 (1967) 374-77, and Rose Graham, *Saint Gilbert of Sempringham and the Gilbertines* (London: 1901). Sempringham is about ten miles southwest of Swineshead, an easy journey on horseback over flat country. Two other priories of Gilbertine nuns were also quite close: Catley, founded in 1148x54 and Haverhome, founded in 1137 (Cistercian) and 1139 (Gilbertine), according to Knowles, *Heads* 201, 202. About Swineshead, Dorothy M. Owen, *Church and Society in Medieval Lincolnshire* (Lincoln, 1971) 152, notes cryptically: 'Swineshead . . . Site known: modern farmhouse'. Hilary Costello, 'Gilbert of Hoyland', *Citeaux* 27 (1976) 109-121, notes that the site of the abbey 'lies about eight miles from the west bank of the Wash. But in the mid-twelfth century the coastline was in places much closer to the abbey, reaching possibly to Sutterton five miles to the southwest'.

38. See S 37:3, S 6:1, S 7:1, S 31:7, S 46:2, S 23:3, also index under 'Cistercian'.

39. For this choice of defects see Mikkers, 38-9, and S 14:7, S 45:3, S 47:8 and S 43:8. A psychological study would indicate Gilbert's insight into some normal problems of monks; see the index e.g. for tedium, which is generally accompanied by sadness, for distaste and disaffection. The greathearted Gilbert understood the foibles of humanity, St Paul's 'weariness in well-doing', the need for freedom of conscience to develop in virtue. Gilbert knew how to throw both the light of understanding and the warmth of loving humor and consolation on his brother monks in temptation and trial. He showed himself both frankly realistic and helpfully approachable. With brother abbots he was a man of the Rule and fearless in telling them what it meant. For a dictionary of *Cistercian Sign Language* as it has survived to the present century, see the book of that title (CS 11, 1975).

40. For his formal treatise on ambition and presumption, see T 7^1; for Brother William, Ep 3; for successors of Roger, T 7^2:10-11; for vain preachers, S 27:2, S 31:4, S 36:6; for a niggardly bursar, T 7^1:5; for the disaffected monk, S 29:7, and the complaining nun, S 17:2. Gilbert questions the actions of Alexander III, whose cause none the less he champions against the anti-pope Victor IV, S 30:8, and see De Lubac, *Exegese* 3:520, n. 5.

41. See T 7^1:6, Bernard also used the word *grunnio,* grunt like swine, harrumph, of the brethren showing disapproval, as Talbot pointed out in *Sermones Inediti B. Aelredi Abbatis Rievallensis,* Series Scriptorum S. Ordinis Cisterciensis, V. 1 (Rome, 1952) p. 7, n. 4: *Bene fecistis grunniendo, significare quod minime ita sapiatis imo quod non ita desipiatis, ne in eo quod planum est immoremur'* (PL 183:970). For the bestiary, see John Morson, 'The English Cistercians and the Bestiary', *Bulletin of John Rylands Library* 39 (1956) 146-170; A. Dimier, 'Menagerie Cistercienne' and 'Heraldique Cistercienne', *Citeaux* 24 (1973) 5-30, 267-282. See T 1:2, for the 'Archpoet'.

42. For the helmet-shaped honeycomb, S 41:5; the busy bee, S 41:6; bees building honeycombs of more perfect and mystic doctrine, S 34:2; green vegetables in a truck garden, S 37:2; the rose ever red, the white lily, the purple violet, S 41:2; the rose amid thorns, S 32:3; the chemist and perfumer with drugs and perfumes, mortar and pestle and cauldron, S 17:6; the scalpel of physician and goldsmith, T 6:9; old silver tarnishing from neglect, S 17:6. The

tailor weaves and measures clothes for the raiment of the Word, S 34:8; the
chandler knows melting wax, how hot it is and how it runs, S 44:4-5, 7; the cobbler and blacksmith know how to turn shoes into a crown, S 21:5; the barber
knows locks and scissors for tonsuring and about baldness, S 23:1-2; the baker
knows about harvesting wheat, and leaven, S 41:7; crumbs from the table, T 3:7.
The spirit veers like a ship in the wind, S 38:6; fishermen know about harbors,
tides, dykes and sluice-gates mentioned so frequently, and the irrigator about
fountains and wells, and the need for well-diggers, S 37:4-5. The plowman appre-
ciated the multiple references to gardens and wheatfields and orchards, as the
cartwright knew the hayrack and the proud carriage, while the scribe remembered the abbot's words: 'If the heart of a man be stretched like a parchment of
the sky, it will fold shut like a book and condense like a mist', T 3:7. The shepherd was alert for butting and attacking, for old wool and new fleece, for sheep-
shearing, to note sheep's teeth white and evenly matched, to know a dog's bark
from its bite, but what would he make of the 'martyrs who were sheep, cropping
their persecutors to store them in the bowels of the church'? S 23:6-8. S 24:1.
For the two nuns, see S 17:2-3; for the birdwatcher, T 7^2:4.

43.   For soldiering see S 16:2; walls and ramparts, S 35:2; towers and outworks, S 35:2; mail, Ep 1:2; helmets, S 41:5; shields, S 26:8; swords and duelling, S 16:4-6.

44.   See Roger Sherman Loomis, *The Grail, from Celtic Myth to Christian
Symbol,* (N. Y.: Columbia U. Press, 1963) 106, 179, 187, 189; A. Pauphilet,
Etude sur la queste del saint Graal, (Paris: 1921); M. Lot-Borodine, 'Les Grands
Secrets du Saint-Graal dans la Lumiere du Graal', *Etudes et texts sous la direction
de Rene Nelli* (Paris, 1951) 151-174, and Irenee Vallery-Radot, 'La Queste del
Saint Graal', Coll. 17 (1955) 201-213; Coll. 18 (1956) 3-20, 199-213, 321-32.

45.   See S 38:1; also H. E. Hallam, *Settlement,* index under *Swineshead,*
and map 6 of south Lincolnshire in 1307; the map gives a good idea of the sweep
of the Wash, the dyking system and Swineshead Abbey not far from Holland Fen
and Holland Dyke which continued eastward to Sykemouth (A syke 'is a tract of
land unfit for tillage', p. 141, n. 1) and New Dyke which may date from 1170; see
R. A. Donkin, 'The marshland holdings of the English Cistercians before c. 1350',
Citeaux 9 (1958) 262-275.

46.   See T 6:4, 9.

47.   T 72:4, on the site of Stocking, for hills and mountains S 28:2-6;
gardens S 35-37; trees, flowers and plants S 36:1-2; S 37:2, S 39:5.

48.   See T 7^2:4; for *denique* introducing RB 33, see Ep 3:1.

49.   S 16:8, S 35:7, S 23:3.

50.   S 47:2.

51.   T 7^1:10.

52.   S 16:4.

53.   Ep 2:3-4.

54.   S 48:1.

55.   S 47:2; G. refers to a decree of the General Chapter of 1137, which
requires the authorization of the General Chapter for writing books: *'Nulli liceat
abbati nec monacho nec novitio libros facere, nisi forte cuiquam in generali abba-
tum capitulo concessum fuerit',* Statuta 1134. LVIII; J. M. Canivez, *Statuta
Capitulorum Generalium Ordinis Cisterciensis* (Louvain: 1933-39) I:26 (cited by
Mikkers).

56.   See S 36:3, for his quotation from Jerome, and Ep 3:6, for his request
for Jerome on Isaiah.

57.   T 5.

58.   S 31:2, S 32:2, S 13:3, also *Prayers and Meditations of St Anselm,*
tr. Benedicta Ward, (Penguin, 1975) 141-56, and Andre Cabussut, 'Une Devotion
peu connue', RAM 25 (1949) 234-45.

59.   Gilson, *Mystical Theology,* 230; see S 37:8, where Gilbert quotes
Is 7:9 (LXX).

60.   Lam, 'Gilbert of Hoyland', in DSp 6 (1967) 373-5. See N. R. Ker, 'Medieval Libraries of Great Britain', *Transactions of the Royal Hist. Soc.* 1962; M. A. Dimier. 'Les premiers cisterciens etaient-ils ennemis des etudes?' *Studia Monastica* 4 (Montferrat: 1962) 69-91; C. H. Talbot, 'The English Cistercians and the Universities', *Studia Monastica* 4 (1962) 197-220; C. R. Cheney, 'English Cistercian Libraries: the first century', *Medieval Texts and Studies* (Oxford: Clarendon, 1973) 328-345; Etienne Gilson, 'Regio Dissimilitudinis de Platon a Saint Bernard de Clairvaux', MS 9 (1947) 108-130.

61.   Gilson, *Mystical Theology,* 230; Mikkers, 40-41; Miquel, 150-159.

62.   Miquel, 158-9.

63.   Gilson, *Mystical Theology,* 231; M.-Andre Fracheboud, 'Divinisation', DSp 3 (1957) 1407-8.

64.   Name of Christ, S 5:10.

65.   Lothaire II, S 30:6.

66.   Barbarossa, S 30:8-9, S 38:4.

67.   Kings T 7^2:2.

68.   Officials, S 45:8.

69.   Mikkers, 42-3; see L. A. Desmond, 'Becket and the Cistercians', *Canadian Catholic Historical Association* 35 (1968) 9-29.

70.   Banquets, T 7^2:4.

71.   Starvation, S 38:1-2.

72.   See Mikkers, 42-43.

73.   Leclercq, *Love of Learning,* 139-184.

74.   *Handbook of Church History,* eds. Hubert Jedin and John Dolan, IV. 'From the High Middle Ages to the Eve of the Reformation', Hans-Georg Back, Karl August Fink, Josef Glazik, Erwin Iserloch, Hans Wolter, tr. Anselm Biggs, (Herder, 1970) 42-43; Gilson, *Mystical Theology,* 63; *Sancti Bernardi Opera* II, *Sermones super Cantica Canticorum,* 33-86, 'Introduction, Observations sur la langue et le style de Saint Bernard', by Christine Mohrmann, ix-xxxiii.

75.   PL 183:1307-8.

76.   S 33:6, and Bernard SC 10ff.

77.   S 22:1, and Bernard SC 40:4 and 45:1-2 and 6.

78.   S 1:7, S 1:2.

79.   S 1:3, S 4:2.

80.   Gilson, *Mystical Theology,* 63.

81.   De Lubac, *Exegese,* 1:94-110, 2:657-667.

82.   S 7:2.

83.   Gilson, *Mystical Theology,* 229.

84.   See CCCM 17, *Joannis de Forda* pp. vii, 33-37; Eric Colledge, *The Mediaevel Mystics of England,* (N. Y.: Scribner's, 1961) 55; for *litterarius sermo* see S 37:7.

85.   Seneca, *Ep. mor.* 9:11. De Lubac, *Exegese Medieval,* 1:595 n. 9, seems to be musing on Gilson's comments on Gilbert in *Mystical Theology,* 230.

86.   S 9:3.

87.   L. Braceland, 'Nuns in the Audience of Gilbert of Hoyland', SMC 11 (1976).

88.   A translation of the Sermons of John of Ford, based on the critical edition of Frs Mikkers and Costello appear in the Cistercian Fathers Series, (Volume I=CF 29, 1977). See E. Mikkers 'Les sermons inedits de Jean de Ford', in Coll. 5 (1938) 250-261; C. J. Holdsworth, 'John of Ford and English Cistercian Writing, 1167-1224', in *Transactions of the Royal Historical Society,* 5th series, 11 (1961) 117-136; A. D., 'John of Ford', in *Citeaux* 21 (1970) 105-110; H. Costello, 'The idea of the Church in the Sermons of John of Ford', *Citeaux* 21 (1970) 236-264, and 'John of Ford and the Quest for Wisdom', *Citeaux* 23 (1972) 141-159. See E. Faye Wilson, 'Pastoral and Epithalamium in Latin Literature', *Speculum* 23 (1948) 35-57, esp. 42-46; A. Robert, R. Tournay,

A. Feuillet, *Le Cantique des Cantiques* (Paris: Gabalda, 1963) 387, 390ff, 432.

89.   T 3:7, *sermocinati sumus*; several times Gilbert calls a sermon a treatise, *tractatus*, though the word may mean the treatment of a text: S 43:9, S 44:1, S 33:1, and *tractaturus eram de transitu sponsae*, S 7:1; for *litterarius sermo*, see S 44:1.

90.   Mikkers discusses the manuscripts, 269-71, and the doubtful or spurious works, 273-79; de Lubac, *Exegese Medieval* 1:126, quotes from a Prologue of an abbot Gilbert on the Gospel according to Matthew, 'whether this be Gilbert of Stanford, Gilbert of Hoyland or some other' and refers to an article of Jean Leclercq in MS 15 (1953) 102-3, which suggests the need of further research and independent evidence for a judgement on these texts.

91.   Bernard Longergan, *Method in Theology* (New York: Herder, 1972) p. 71.

GILBERT OF HOYLAND

Volume One

ON THE
SONG OF SONGS I

TEXT

SERMON 1
PEACE AND LEISURE

The lover's quest for God requires peace and leisure: 1. the affections of lovers prompt varied outcries, which defy logical order; 2-3. the quest, the touch, the embrace, presuppose the peace of the little bed of the night; 4. the day of man and the day of God are at odds; 5. good is the night which hides from us the sight of the ephemeral world; 6. but many are those nights because interrupted by the daylight of his presence; 7. bad and good conscience differ in their love of the Beloved; 8. why the word 'soul' is so frequent in the canticle of love.

IN MY LITTLE BED BY NIGHT, I SOUGHT HIM WHOM MY SOUL LOVES[1]*   **Sg 3:1*

The affections of lovers are subject to change, for their situations are subject to change. So the cries of the bride at times seem disjointed, for now according to her longing she enjoys her Beloved but again contrary to her longing she is bereft of him. In the preceding verse she invites him to return over the mountains, but here in her little bed she seeks him when he has slipped away. What link will you propose for this sequence of events? What link in logic is to be pointed out? Rather than a link there seems to be a break in logic. The longings of love are not of one form. So their expression is not bound by a chain of

logic. In love affection blurts out, then checks its
words, for affection does not always remain in one
self-consistent mood. Even the Bridegroom himself is
compared to a fawn, and rightly, because he so
deludes, so eludes his beloved. Hence the change in
her lacks neither sequence nor logic. Her cries,
though changing so suddenly, do not break the link
as long as they echo her changed affections.

Examine now amid change the links in the chain
of her longings.[2] Like a fawn carefree and nimble, he
had .skipped over the mountain away from his
beloved; she in turn slipped back into herself from
the mountains whereon she had been wondrously
enlightened and illumined by the sight of her
Beloved; from the mountains, yes she slipped back
into her bed of grief in the valley of tears, into her
bed and into the night from the mountains of light.
Why should she not so withdraw, when her Beloved
has so withdrawn? For in person he is the life and the
light of his bride. So at his retreat, she retreats to her
little bed of infirmity and to her night of unknowing.
At last she tosses upon her couch of infirmity. Upon
her couch however, she recalls her Beloved. Not now
at dawning but at night she meditates on him,[3] seeking the one her soul loves. Not indolent is her action
in this bed on which she has fallen. She is not wanton
nor does she dally on a bed of concupiscence; but she
struggles the more, mindful of her only Beloved, van-
quished not by infirmity but by charity. Whoever
approves this interpretation, may adopt it.

Personally, however, I do not here accept the bed
as one of grief, unless perhaps of that grief which
love begets for an absent spouse, for the bride seems
to wish to be allured rather than to be cured and to
have sought a friend rather than a physician. With
my interpretation you can proceed as follows: from
the mountains he hurried to the little bed of his
bride where she, first aroused and then swooning
under the largess of delight, fell asleep exhausted in
the embrace of her Beloved. She slumbered in sweet
sleep, but awakened, this lady of delights did not find
him in her arms. So those joys, inexpressible joys,

passing over in silence, at last she breaks into this
cry: 'In my little bed by night I sought him whom
my soul loves'. About the link with the previous
verse, let this now suffice.

2. Next let us weigh her words one by one: 'on
my little bed by night I sought him whom my soul
loves'. It is enchanting enough to seek you, good
Jesus, but more enchanting to hold you.[4] The
former is a devout task, the latter sheer joy. To
embrace you is surely enchanting, for your very
touch is rewarding. The woman of the Gospel by a
happy ruse touched the hem of Jesus' garment and at
once the flow of blood was staunched,* that flow of   *Lk 8:44.*
carnal attraction, of carnal licentiousness and anxiety.
The fluid once coursing through her was dammed
and dried up and all this she accomplished through
the touch of his garment. What if she had succeeded
in embracing his person? Not only would the flow
have been staunched and the blood congealed, but
there would have been an overflow of that gushing
stream which refreshes the city of God.* Good then   *Ps 45:5.*
is a touch, but an embrace is better. In a crowd, in
public, with difficulty is Jesus touched. So the bride
who longs not only to touch but also to enfold and
embrace the Word of life, shuns the public and seeks
the privacy of her little bed at night.

A good work it is either to seek or to hold Jesus,
but for this work a suitable time and place must be
found. What better place than one's little bed, what
time more fitting than by night, for the exercise of
love? Only with a calm mind can one seek the delight
of wisdom, for with a restless gaze one cannot focus
upon her. Nothing defiled* and indeed nothing wild   *Ws 7:25.*
hastens to her. But into a spirit restful and pure,
on her own, wisdom is wont to hasten and enter
gratuitously. For in peace is her place and her dwelling is in Sion,* that is in contemplation.[5] How will   *Ps 75:3.*
an eye irritated by anger or anxiety gaze upon the
unapproachable light which is penetrated only by
a clear mind and not always at its own good pleasure?

What then has peace to do with a little bed, you
ask. Much indeed, in the sense that, as in a little bed

so no less in peace, one sleeps and rests. As the psalmist says: 'In peace in the self-same I shall sleep and rest'.[6] Why should a holy soul not willingly rest where her Beloved has his place? For in peace is his place. So first win this place for yourself, that there you may entertain your soul's Beloved when he slips in or thence seek him when he slips out. For in one's little bed and in the mind's hidden retreat, he can be traced more freely, found more quickly, held more securely and perhaps detained for a longer spell, if indeed any spell be long in delights which practically at their inception are wont to be interrupted. For the bride too, swooning as it were in the midst of embraces and then pursuing these fleeting delights, again fretfully seeks her beloved and seeks him in her little bed.

You too are in a good place upon your bed, if in leisure your mind is freely relaxed from its labors. What is more suited to the exercise of love than freedom and leisure? For freedom engenders attraction and in leisure affection is likewise liberated and awarded no little assistance. This is beyond dispute. The more the spirit is freed from harness, the more it will hasten towards what it loves. In practice, whenever we recover our leisure, then we feel the more keenly the spur of divine love. Contrariwise, frequent preoccupation with the world almost blunts the affections and makes the spirit callous.[7] Preoccupation entangles, repose unravels the spirit. If disentangled, to what heights do you think our desires might range?

3. Do you see how many blessings may be stored in a little bed? Repose, freedom, affectivity. For on the little bed of repose and respite, longings burn the more ardently. A place suited to the charm of charity prompts the bride to seek more ardently. For there she is bereft of her beloved with greater anguish, where she could enjoy him with greater fruitfulness. 'On my little bed' she says, and 'by night'. Because she seeks him by night, in my view her quest is less for the sight of him than for his embrace. She desires rather to hold him than to behold him. To behold is

indeed good, but to enfold unites more intimately, for 'he who clings to the Lord becomes one spirit with him'.* Yet both actions together are better, for then they enrich each other in turn with increase of grace.

    1 Co 6:17.

If you think you are unlikely to attain both, make yours the quest of the bride: seek the embraces of the Beloved. The night of your unknowing, or rather the nights of your unknowings, rob you of the clear vision of heavenly mysteries. Seek consolations; seek to experience them, if you cannot know them. Night does not inhibit delights, for sometimes it is illuminated by them, for 'night' says the psalmist, 'is my illumination in my delights'.* 'In my delights' he says, not 'in knowledge'. Endeavor then, to illumine the night if not with knowledge then with delights. Whatever we see on earth in a mirror and in riddles, all is in the night. Even in this night my Jesus can be more gently experienced with tender affection than known face to face.[8] Though one be not yet admitted to his sight, still by seeking the Beloved in one's bed by night, one may try to embrace him.

    Ps 138:11.

4. What if night also contributes to the discovery of the Beloved? For night does collaborate and very appositely. As you interpret the little bed to be the leisure of holy repose, so consider the night to be a kind of forgetfulness.[9] Each provides an occasion for the exchange of wisdom and contemplation. Solomon wishes you to write of wisdom only in time of leisure, while Paul strains forward to what lies ahead only when he has forgotten what lies behind.* Are you surprised that the night is good and the day evil? 'The day of man' says the prophet, 'I have not desired'.* Somehow the day of the Lord and the day of man are opposed to each other and each hides itself in the other, for when one dawns the other fades away. 'I have not desired the day of man', that is the applause of men, human glory, to appear respected among others, even above others. Rightly the prophet renounces this day, because it provides a source of disturbance. Better than the day then, is this night, since night conceals a man from

    Si 38:25;
    Phm 3:13.

    Jr 17:16.

the disturbance to which the day exposes him. In
Genesis, as soon as our first parents opened their

Gn 3:7.

eyes to this daylight, they blushed in confusion.*
How much happier were they previously when they
kept their eyes closed, and when under cover of a
better night, they knew not sin's concupiscence!
Thence this evil day drew its origin, for it laid bare
the paths of vice, exposed alluring shapes and
presented fascinating objects to the eye of concupiscence.

Alas, how this day glitters around me, how it
ensnares my affection! In what a naked light and
how importunately do wild and lascivious images
parade before the eyes of the mind! There is
practically nowhere to turn aside, nowhere to hide;
no hiding place is secure enough. From all sides there
break and emerge into consciousness, whether deli-
berately welcomed or lightly brushed aside, all the
images which trouble and defile the spirit. For
though the spirit with stricter resolution may repel
them, still it is sullied by the mere touch of these
marauding thoughts. 'Whoever touches pitch shall

Si 13:1.

be defiled by it.'* According to the statutes of the
Law, even the slightest touch of some objects causes

Lv 4:8.

defilement.* Such thoughts, since they are introduced by force, are not charged to our account and
do not imply guilt, though they inflict some harm
on the purity to which we aspire. What results when
images of the body pour into a contemplative spirit?
Perhaps they do not arouse carnal desire, but they do
impede spiritual vision. Some images trouble, others
defile, others impede; that is they wound, allure or
deceive. Would not everything of the kind be better
concealed than illustrated,[10] cloaked in the blind
shadow of oblivion rather than catalogued by heart?

5. Good then is the night which in discreet
forgetfulness disguises all things ephemeral, schedul-
ing a time and providing an occasion to seek him
who is eternal. Good is the night which conceals the
concupiscence of the world, its anxiety, its thoughts.
This is indeed to keep the world hidden or to be
hidden from the world. We also can be so concealed

in the shelter of your presence, O Lord,* I do not
say with full knowledge, but with all devotion and
free enquiry and some discovery. Our withdrawal,
our concealment, our hiding-places, by which we shun
either the love or the fancy of worldly daylight and
by which we do not retrieve the world's day once
abandoned and scorn the world's day when proffered,
these in my opinion, are here termed night by the
bride. For in an earlier verse she says: 'I sat beneath
the shadow of him whom I desired and his fruit was
sweet to my palate'.*

Ps 30:21

S 2:3.

His fruit gives tasty nourishment, provided his
shadow has previously given cover. Good is his shadow, which conceals the prudence of the flesh and
chills concupiscence. Do you understand the meaning of shadow? The passage offers you a brilliant
pretext to consider 'shadow' and 'night' as synony-
mous, except that some hiding-places, better screened
and camouflaged, more suited to the exercise of
enquiry and contemplation, are expressed by the
word 'night' rather than by 'shadow'. By the word
'shadow' understand some forgetfulness of the visible
world and by the word 'night' total oblivion. Who will
grant me so to progress towards the dusk? Who, I
ask, will grant that my remembrance of an ephemeral world may fade into the dusk of this oblivion?
Good indeed is the night when empty phantasies
neither torment the spirit nor flutter within it, when
they are concealed from the eyes of one seeking the
Beloved. Perfect love itself entices this night, for
it neither notices nor acknowledges as acquaintances
the rest of the world, as long as it sighs without distraction for him it loves.

6. 'By night', says the bride. Her nights are many;
hers is not one single night, continuous and uninterrupted. Frequently her nights are graced by the
presence of the Bridegroom. His presence is daylight;
his absence is night. So for the bride her nights are
many, since the Bridegroom often eludes her, often
goes into hiding. Obviously blessed is the bride who
clings to her Beloved each livelong day and seeks him
throughout each long-lived night. Let her actions, as

you hear of them, prompt your rivalry and, taught
by the example of the bride, do you also 'arise in the
night, in the beginning of your vigils, and pour out
Lm 2:19.   your heart',* that it may melt and flow and run even
to the sight of your God. To him consecrate the
beginnings of your vigils; let no errant distractions
pluck a moment of your self.

Seek your Beloved each and every night. Why do I
say each and every night? Throughout every single
livelong night persevere throughout this task. Do not
pause and do not rest until your Beloved rises like the
Is 62:1.   dawn and is enkindled for you like a wedding-torch.*
Then you can sing the verse of St Paul: 'the night is
far gone, the day is at hand', although his next verse,
Rm 13:12.   'let us then cast off the works of darkness',* cannot be
applied to a night such as this. For this night knows
not the works of darkness, but rather holds a torch
for those who persevere in the race in quest of the
Beloved.[11] Good indeed is the night when you are
hidden from the riot and the assault of fantasies. And
though you are not yet hidden in the shelter of your
Beloved's presence, still it is good that from you is concealed the ostentatious presence of vain and carnal
thoughts. Night falls that you may not notice, may
not see that presence. Still in this night your lamp will
not be extinguished that you may seek your Beloved.

7. Would that I might enumerate as my own
such nights, so concealing and so revealing! Who
among us will boast that all his nights are so spent?
Happy the man whoever he is, if all his nights fly past
in such . exercise and who in private does nothing
which requires concealment. Let every one consult
his own conscience. Why should I wound the con-
1 Co 8:12.   science of another, if it is weak?* I neither wound
nor probe such a conscience. Weak though it. be, at
least let it not be corrupt. Let conscience not enact or
even think in private what it is indecent even to mention. The sickbed of such a conscience Jesus knows
not how to visit. A shameful conscience insults him
and chases him off. The blush of a guilty conscience,
far from beckoning him, rather dodges him. What
seeks him however is charity arising from a pure

heart and a good conscience.* This is confirmed by
our verse: 'I sought him whom my soul loves'.
Nothing is more secure than a good conscience. A
good conscience is bold for its love is not cold; it lives
without fright, for love sets it alight; it does not
blush before the Beloved, for love trusts the Beloved.
Great is the power of love. It does not rely on another's favor but is satisfied with its own deserts.
Conscious that it loves, it assumes that it always
loved. In the Canticle, disregarding his other titles of
distinction, the bride mentions only her 'Beloved',
because in a special way she endures within the ardor
of his love.

8. Notice how frequently, whatever the mystery,
she recalls the word 'Beloved'. 'My Beloved is radiant
and ruddy', and 'Such is my Beloved',* and in the
present verse, 'whom my soul loves'. Great assuredly
is the charm of this word. It is no surprise if what
glows in her heart overflows from her lips. In the
same way also she reflects on her soul. For she loves
not only in word but also in her heart, not in deed
alone but especially in affection. Now what is meant
by her mention of 'soul' rather than 'spirit'? Perhaps
she did not yet cling to her Beloved whom she was
still seeking, for 'he who clings to the Lord is one
spirit with him'.* Indeed nowhere in the entire Canticle does she use the word 'spirit', but she says, 'My
soul melted' and 'my soul was troubled' and, frequently in the present verse, 'he whom my soul
loves'.* Even this verse she almost never uses, except
when she seeks him in his absence or complains of
his absence.

By these terms several degrees of perfection are
differentiated: a soul more perfect and a soul less
perfect. The apostle says: 'An unspiritual man does
not receive the gifts of the Spirit of God'.[12]
Personally I would never call unspiritual this soul,[13]
so ardently in love, so fervent in her quest, for though
still without full vision yet with ever increasing desire,
she clings to him whom she passionately loves. But
as we can aptly consider 'spirit' to mean a subtle and
refined understanding, so we can consider 'soul' to

1 Tm 1:5.

Sg 5:10, 5:16.

1 Co 6:17.

Sg 5:6, 6:11, 3:1.

Ezk 11:19.

Jb 6:12.

Heb 4:12.

mean a gentle and tender affection. The Lord
promises us through the prophet: 'I will give you a
heart of flesh'.* If then in some passage, the word
'flesh' can be understood in a good sense, why not
still more the word 'soul'? In calling this soul
blessed without reservation, personally I would consider hers a soul of flesh rather than of stone, possess-
ing neither stubbornness nor harshness, but soft,
tender, pliant, and sensitive to each and every arrow
from the divine Word. Indeed with Job she may
say 'not of bronze is my flesh',* but through it a
sword of the spirit may pass and she may rejoice in
having been wounded by charity.* Rightly then does
the bride claim that her soul is in love, for she desires
to express her intimate, vivid and lively affection
towards her beloved Lord, Jesus Christ, who lives
and reigns for ever and ever. Amen.

NOTES TO SERMON ONE

1.   G. addresses one individual throughout (*videte* of par. 2 needs emendation to *vide tu* or *videsne*). He discusses the link between Sg 2:17 and Sg 3:1, as if continuing his own oral or written comments on Sg 1-2. The key words of his first sentence, the affections of lovers, *affectus amantium* are found in Seneca, *Ep. mor.* 9:11. For *'hinnulus,* the fawn or young stag, see T. H. White, *The Bestiary,* (N.Y.: Putnam's, 1960), p. 39, hereafter cited as White.

Although G. does not mention Bernard, his Sermons first overlap and then continue Bernard, who commented on Sg 3:1-4 in SC 75-79, and returned for further reflections on Sg 3:1 in SC 80-86. At Bernard's death in 1153, G. who had already been an abbot for some three to six years, was apparently already giving an oral and/or a written explanation of the Canticle for his monks. Encouraged or commissioned to publish (see Mikkers 267, and G. S 47:2), he seems to have continued his own work from a natural break at the beginning of Sg 3:1. Bernard's manner and style, which G. is credited with following, is discussed by Christine Mohrmann, 'Observations sur la langue et le style de Saint Bernard', SBOp II, ix-xxxv, and by Jean Leclercq in the intro. to CF 7, vii-xxx, with references to G. p. xix. G's first eight sermons form a group which he summarizes in the last paragraph of S 8: the bride searches until she finds the Bridegroom; in his next group of sermons, S 9-14, he stops to dwell on the scene as the bride holds the Bridegroom *tenui eum . . .* Sg 3:4. In his third group of sermons, S 15-21, G. actually addresses or uses the literary device of addressing a group of nuns, as he explains the words of the chorus of the 'daughters of Jerusalem' in the Canticle, Sg 3:6-11.

2.   On affection of the heart, see Jean Chatillon *cordis affectus* in DSP 2 (1953) 2280-2300.

3.   Ps 62:1, 6; enumeration of the Vulgate is followed throughout for the Psalms. On 'memory of blessings' see P. Debongnie, 'Meditation des Bienfaits de Dieu', in DSp 1 (1937) 1608-18.

4.   *Bone Jesu,* the most frequent apostrophe to the Lord in G.; this and the following sentences are cited by St Bonaventure and attributed to St Bernard according to Lam; see *Comment. in Ev. Lucae,* c. 8, *Opera omnia,* (Quaracchi, 1895) 7:211.

5.   See Jean Leclercq, 'Vocabulaire monastique', 82-85, under *speculatio,* and de Lubac, *Exegese Medieval* 2 (1959) 633.

6.   Ps 4:9. Bellarmine on the Psalms, (Paris: Vives, ed, 1861) cites Jerome and others who translate *idipsum* as the 'self-same' but Augustine who translates it as 'God' as in Ps 101:12, 27, 28. See also Aug. *Med.* v. 22, c. 37, p. 621 (Paris: Vives, 1861); I owe the reference to Fr Ambrose Davidson OCSO.

7.   The metaphor is from classical Latin, e.g. Seneca, Quintilian; Cicero writes *callum ducere animo,* but G. *menti,* a word not distinguishable in meaning

from *animum* in his next line. G. disguises his knowledge of classical authors.

8.   See G. S 2:8, S 23:1. See Miquel p. 154, n. 13.

9.   Leclercq, *Otia Monastica*, pp. 128-9 n. 67, notes in comparison with others, particularly with William of St Thierry, the great frequency of G.'s words of repose; see Lam, 'Le Monastere: foyer de vie spirituelle', Coll. 26 (1964) 21 n. 90 for *quies*, n. 91 for *otium*, n. 91 for *lectulus*, n. 93 for *vacatio*.

10.   Add *esset*, as noted in Mabillon and Migne.

11.   1 Co 9:25, 2 Tm 2:5, third antiphon of the first nocturn for the Octave of All Saints: *Sanctum est verum lumen et admirabile, ministrans lucem his qui permanserunt in agone certaminis.* For liturgical texts in G. see Lam 'Les observances monastiques: instruments de vie spirituelle', Coll. 26 (1964) 171 n. 8; hereafter Lam.

12.   1 Co 2:14, *Animalis autem homo non percipit ea quae sunt Spiritus Dei.* Here G. distinguishes the *anima* in *animalis homo,* the vital principle of the body, from the *spiritus,* a higher aspect of the *anima,* which can be united with the Spirit of God.

13.   Mab. reads *animam meam* where G. means the *anima mea* in his text; Migne changes *animam meam* to *animam hanc* for clarity.

*Resting, the lover restlessly seeks the Beloved.
1. The narrow bed of the heart does not
welcome an adulterer with the Beloved. 2. What
is the little bed of conscience? How passing
and slight are peace and liberty of mind in
this body! 3. The night means not fear but
hope in the Lord. 4. The little bed has three
senses like three degrees of contemplative
prayer; 5. in her bed love yields neither to
weakness of nature not to adversity (an interpretation appropriate for religious). 6. At rest,
love never rests until she finds her little bed in
the Beloved; 7. he is the little bed for little ones,
the nest for fledglings by his cross and crown;
8. morally, the occasion, the action, and the
motive for love are here.*

IN MY LITTLE BED BY NIGHT, I SOUGHT HIM
WHOM MY SOUL LOVES.*   *Sg 3:1.*

F rom yesterday's passage, let me celebrate
with you the banquet for today. For not all
was said there which appears worth saying;
some points were not even touched. In this
sermon let us take up two points worth discussion:
why does the bride say 'in a little bed' and not in 'a
bed', and why 'in my little bed', for elsewhere she
was wont to say 'in our little bed'.*   *Sg 1:16.*
Count these
points as your principal; if, however, I add some
fresh insights into topics already discussed, consider

this a kind of interest. What hidden meaning is implied, do you suppose, in the bride's words, 'in a little bed'? Does the phrase conceal some suggestion of praise or of blame? Though the diminutive can imply either alternative, here however I am more ready to adopt the suggestion of praise. Let us turn our discussion, then, first to this interpretation.

Clearly in the diminutive I understand some narrowing, so that the little bed is large enough for only the Beloved with the bride. Why not interpret narrowing in a good sense, if a widening of the couch is turned into a reproach? 'You have spread wide your couch', the Lord says through the prophet, 'you have welcomed an adulterer beside me'.[1] You see how, with rebuke and reproach, the expansion of her couch is charged against the adulterous soul. It is good then not to expand but rather to contract the couch of one's thought and the little bed of one's heart. Rightly then the bride congratulates herself on her little bed. 'The couch is so narrow', says Isaiah, 'that the one or the other may fall out and the short blanket cannot cover both'.* 'Both' means the husband and the adulterer. Indeed the heart of man is confined and narrow in welcoming the delights of God's Word, even when his heart is wide open for those delights.[2] Will not your heart be much more confined, if it is opened wide to other pleasures? However confined it may be, let it be shared only by your Beloved. Do not make narrowness more narrow by sharing your little bed with another.

Is 28:20.

Good is the confinement of this little bed which knows how to welcome only its Beloved, that is, Christ alone. Indeed there is a narrowness which knows how to welcome him only, and a narrowness which is unable to welcome him fully. The former is characteristic of charity and discipline, but the latter of natural weakness. Both kinds of narrowness can be understood of the little bed, either that whereby the bed excludes other lovers than the Beloved, or that whereby the bed cannot include him fully. Certainly great is the pleasure of the little bed but great also its narrowness; therefore with good reason is it called 'little bed' rather than 'bed'.

2. Delightful is the little bed of which one reads in Proverbs: 'A carefree mind is a perpetual feast'.* *Pr 15:15.* Outside is the night, outside the hurricane, but inside tranquillity like a little bed of repose. There is no need to repeat here the lament: 'Outside the sword slays and indoors is like death'.* Rather, if outside is *Lm 1:20.* a sword, inside is rejoicing: 'Rejoicing in hope', says the apostle, 'patient under tribulation'.* Tribulation *Rm 12:12.* is attributed to the night, hope and rejoicing to the little bed. Perhaps for this reason the bride says not a 'bed' but a 'little bed', the diminutive term, because practically all our rejoicing is still in hope and imperfect. Good then is the little bed, repose and purity of conscience. The heart of the wicked is like a raging sea which cannot rest; his waves churn up the mire and muck. Thus the heart of the wicked is storm-tossed, wasting away, muddy and ever wrestling with itself. There is no peace for the wicked,* whereas the *Is 57:20-1.* kingdom of God is justice and peace.* 'In peace in *Rm 14:17.* the self-same', says the psalmist, 'I shall sleep and take my rest; you Lord, have specially confirmed me in hope'.* *Ps 4:9, 10.*

The word 'hope' contains both the little bed and rejoicing, for in hope we rejoice and in hope we take our rest. But whence comes hope save from the assurance of conscience? With good reason I would call the little bed a mind assured and free: assured because of a good conscience but free from temptation, free from exterior occupations, free from frivolous thoughts. How much liberty and peace of mind can exist in this body of ours? Slight liberty and brief peace, as if on a narrow little bed. Much of our freedom and repose is filched by our need for bodily refreshment; much by our anxiety to provide necessities, by the time devoted to meals, by some disaster threatening the soul, and by causes still undetected. 'One thing is our boast', says Paul, 'the evidence of our conscience'.* Truly he had placed *2 Co 1:12.* himself on a pleasant little bed. 'I have nothing on my conscience', he says. But the more he enlarges and extends one side the more he narrows and

contracts the other: 'But that does not mean that
I stand acquitted. My judge is the Lord'.* You see
how Paul makes bold to say, 'Our heart has been
opened wide'.* You see how his respect for the
judgement of God restrains the boast and witness
of his conscience.

3. Rightly then is the little bed a mind untroubled but nowise proud; quiet, not puffed up,
having an honest appreciation of itself without
straining for ideas beyond it,* but rather keeping
itself ever on guard against the night of the un-
predictable judgement. 'In my little bed by night'
says the bride; many a night but one little bed, for
'many are the tribulations of the righteous'.* Yet as
if unaware and unheeding, 'they sleep and take their
rest' in one little bed, in that one hope of our vocation in which we have been called.* Night after night
passes, but they do not abandon the little bed of
their tranquillity 'until all iniquity passes away'.*
Many are the nights and deep the darkness, yet they
are not afraid or alarmed at the depth of night,
because they hope in the Lord. They are in no fear
of the nights who rest in the little bed of this hope.
For God too knows how to inspire songs in the night
of tribulation and by night he sends his canticle.*
Now you have learned why the bride speaks of
nights and why in the plural, and why she speaks of a
'little bed' and why in the singular.

4. Next learn why she calls the bed 'mine'. Yes,
hers in the singular, her single bed as long as she is
singularly established in hope.* But when reality
approaches or better displaces hope, when at last
though partially she holds the Beloved, then this
little bed of the bride is no longer hers but shared
instead by Bridegroom and bride. Hers it is when she
reposes alone without the Beloved; shared it is when
he is present. It is the bride's own when with calm,
peaceful, and composed behavior, in self-awareness
she takes her rest. It is shared when she begins at last
to find her delight in the Bridegroom.

Perhaps there is also a bed reserved for the Bridegroom alone, when his beloved, wholly forgetful of

1 Co 4:4.

2 Co 6:11.

Rm 12:16.

Ps 33:20.

Eph 4:4.

Ps 56:2.

Jb 35:10. Ps 41:9.

Ps 4:10.

herself and stripped of herself, passes wholly into him and is, as it were, robed in him.[3] In her own little bed she neither flows out of herself nor is she storm-tossed within herself. In the shared little bed some waves of delight flow over her from the presence of the Bridegroom. In the bed reserved for the Bridegroom alone,[4] melting in the fire of the Bridegroom's love she bubbles up and overflows as liquid and vapor. She flows wholly into him and is absorbed into a similar quality.[5] In her own bed she is at home alone; in the shared bed the Bridegroom is at home with her; in his bed she is entirely at home with him and, if one may say so, there exists no one but the Beloved. In the first bed she seeks him, in the second she clings to him, in the third she is united with him. In the first she possesses her own tranquility, in the second she merits some sharing with her Beloved, in the third she is assumed and absorbed into some union of charity and grace. This third little bed is better than the second, to the extent that union is more intimate than sharing. Yet even the first is good, for it opens the way to the others.

5. But if you prefer to interpret the bed as the enticements of carnal weakness, you make no mistake and present no difficulty in developing that sense. In this sense the little bed belongs to the bride alone and is not shared with the Bridegroom. Although we know Christ according to the flesh, we do not know him according to the concupiscence of the flesh. He does indeed share with us a nature of flesh but not the enticements of the flesh. He did not decline the bed of our pain but he did not recline as far as to feel our pleasure. So when the bride refers to the little bed, in your interpretation she says 'on my bed' and not 'on our bed', not one shared in common. True, we do read in another passage, 'Our bed is all flowers'.* The bed they share is all flowers with nothing of age, nothing of corruption. But when she speaks of her own bed, there is no mention of a flower. It is all the bride's own but it is far from fragrant; to her it seems full not of blossoms but of brambles. A sorry enough plight is this, even were it

Sg 1:16.

no more than corruption, but in fact hardship is added to weakness and the distress is doubled: the little bed and the night, weakness and hardship. Yet great is the power of love for neither of these can vanquish love, neither inborn weakness nor inflicted hardship. She is neither imprisoned by her bed nor terrified by the night but 'upon her bed and night after night she seeks him whom her soul loves'.

This verse seems most characteristic of cloistered brethren, because untroubled by anxiety they have their tiny cot and because lost and hidden in a crowd they enjoy the obscurity of the night. However unusual some brother's way of life may be, it is somehow hidden when the sum total of the brethren rises to an equal height, according to the prophecy about our Saviour: 'They walk in darkness and for them there is no light', that is no light of human praise, that the more freely 'they may hope in the name of the Lord and rely upon their God'.* Their 'countenance is hidden . . . . Wherefore we think nothing of them',* especially since interiorly they think nothing of themselves and exteriorly do not adapt themselves to the ways of the world. They are not avid for glory from the lips of men but only for the glory which comes from God, as we read in John, 'I do not seek my own glory', and in Paul, 'Let him who glories glory in the Lord'.* That is to say, let him not acquiesce in the applause of men rather than in the gifts of the Lord. Let him not adulterate in anything the joys of spiritual glory by an admixture of human applause but let him be grateful to the Lord and seek glory in him, for this is to seek the Lord. Such a one has tranquillity as his cot and humility as his night. Gnawing cares do not flutter around him and attacks of restlessness do not provoke him; but for him all is his cot and the night; all is peace and repose and retirement.*

6. Is this enough? Enough perhaps for a laborer but not for a lover. Sweet indeed is sleep to the laborer.* But a lover's fretfulness does not allow him to sleep; it dispels drowsiness and brings on wakefulness. Love is made more restless by rest itself.

Marginalia:
Is 50:10;
Lam 13, n. 48.

Is 53:3.

Jn 8:50; 2 Co 10:
17; Lam 14,
nn. 50, 51.

Lam 20, n. 86.

Qo 5:11.

Temptation rests, business rests, distress rests, but love knows not how to rest. Then its sweet fire grows more vigorous and its devouring flame emerging from its hiding-place ranges more freely through the relaxed spirit, penetrating more deeply and consuming more hungrily. Welcoming its chance, love cannot but practise its craft. Love always either enjoys the Beloved when present or yearns for him when absent.

'In the day of my distress', says the psalm, 'I sought God with outstretched hands'.* Far different is the motive for quest which the bride now proposes. Distress does not drive her but affection draws her. The sage in the psalm seeks the Lord to counter his distress; the bride seeks her Beloved for the encounter and delight of love. Yes, both the little bed of repose and the hiding-place of night refer to this, that she may constantly recall her Beloved, calmly savor his wisdom and taste his sweetness. Therefore much more compelling is the motive for search in one enamored than in one in need, though one can rightly claim that with a kind of holy greed love is always in need. Ever on fire for deeper mysteries and disregarding its present possessions, love tumbles forward head over heels to what lies ahead and like a living hoop, light-heartedly, bounds upward with all its might to the heights, scarcely touching the earth. Even in Paul, love does not consider that it has reached the goal; pressing onward to what lies ahead Paul follows like an animated wheel where the spirit of burning desire sweeps him forward.* On good evidence, 'when a man reaches his goal, he has just begun'.* In our text also, although the bride possesses her little bed, not content with this she seeks her Beloved the more ardently. He is her little bed and her Beloved: her little bed when he supports her in weakness and weariness; her Beloved when he enkindles and sets her ablaze. Little bed and Beloved is he, because she takes her rest in him, because she yearns for and sinks into him.

7. Are you surprised that I call him a little bed?

Ps 76:3.

Ph 3:15.
Si 18:6.

I will make bold to call him something more commonplace or rather more sublime, beyond all the glory for which he is praised. For the more commonplace the things he did for me, the greater evidence he gave me of his goodness. He is a little bed for little ones and a nest for fledglings: 'For the sparrow has found a house for herself and the turtledove a nest where she may lay her young'.* Do you wish to learn what kind of nest? Cast your thoughts, featherless as yet and weak, on the Lord and he will nurture you, until Christ is formed and strengthened in you and you grow to the perfect man who cannot waver.

Rightly therefore is he a little bed who for me by God was made justice and peace and redemption and wisdom.* Who will grant me to be snug in such a little bed? Who, I ask you, will grant me that pillows and bolsters like his may be fastened beneath my elbows and head?* Happy the bolsters which the bride lays beneath her: 'His left arm is under my head and his right will embrace me'.* His left arm she already possesses, his right she promises herself. She holds his left arm but seeks his right, 'for there are delights at your right hand for ever'.* From her little bed she stretches as it were to another little bed.

The softest of pillows for me, good Jesus, is that crown of thorns from your head. A welcome little bed is that wood of your Cross.[6] On this I am born and bred, created and recreated, and upon the altars of your Passion I gladly rebuild for myself the nest of memory. If, however, one is allowed to experience greater and deeper mysteries of your divine Majesty, that does not differ from the little bed and the night, if one regards the fullness to come rather than a small model of human perfection. For whatever in us is more perfect, is still imperfect and to speak more exactly is as yet scarcely a beginning. Accordingly we are called 'some beginning of God's creation'* and described as having received only 'the firstfruits of the Spirit'.*

8. I may perhaps seem foolhardy in trying to explain mysteries not experienced, even concerning the little bed of the bride, for perhaps she built it too

Margin references:

Ps 83:4.

1 Co 1:30.

Ezk 13:18, 20.

Sg 2:6.

Ps 15:11.

Jm 1:18.
Rm 8:23.

delicately and too secretly beyond the reach of our conjectures.[7] Therefore let us descend from mysteries to morals and say that to seek the Bridegroom 'on one's little bed' and 'night after night' means that after the heart has been in turmoil and the flesh disturbed, forgetful of rest and of present delights we try to capture some foretaste of the delights of future sweetness. In this passage then, to sum up in three words, you have an occasion, an action, and a motive. The motive is in the lover, the action in the seeker, while opportunity and occasion are suggested in the little bed and the night. The passage is brief, however, for good is the little bed in which the weary mind gathers fire-wood or rather à blazing fire, wherein love encountering no obstacle more fervently engages in the discipline of desire. But at last let us too rest here a while, and may it be on that little bed on which the bride, while she rested sought her Beloved. So we may learn by our own actual experience what we are now attempting to teach others: how sweet it is to rest in this little bed and to seek the Beloved, Jesus Christ our Lord.

NOTES TO SERMON TWO

1.   Is 57:8. G. uses the second person plural up to this point; in the same person he adds two further sentences, the last of par. 3, and the first of par. 4.

2.   The final letter in three lines in this column of Migne (18A, 18D) have dropped out; read *illas (delicias)* for *illa, corpore* for *corpor* and *lectulo* for *lectul.*

3.   For 'recollection' see Lam p. 190, n. 131, who sees here a parallel with the three degrees of contemplation in Gregory the Great, *Hom. in Ez.*; PL 76:989D.

4.   The comma should follow *solius est sponsi.*

5.   . . . *in similem absorbetur qualitatem,* throws light on: *ipsa [anima] . . . non est nisi ipsę* [sponsus] in S 3:4. Gilson, *Mystical Theology,* 251, n. 292, sees here an 'identity of likeness', analogous to the divinization of man in Bernard, Dil, 9:28, and in William of St. Thierry, Ep frat 2:3:16. See also M.-Andre Fracheboud, 'Divinisation', DSp 3:1407-8.

6.   ' . . . Gilbert of Hoyland, who interpreted the name Galahad as a reference to Christ, equated in his second sermon the bed of Solomon with the Cross of Christ', R. S. Loomis, *The Grail* (N.Y.: Columbia U. Press, 1963) 187.

7.   Precisely on this paragraph, Gilson rests the proof of his statement: 'Gilbert was not a great mystic, perhaps no mystic at all . . . and in his commentary he prudently remains on the level of the 'moral interpretation'. But he has a strong and well-poised mind, and his writings are well worth reading', *Mystical Theology,* 230, n. 75. Mikkers, 40, n. 3, thinks Gilson has been too harsh in his judgement and Miquel comes gently to G.'s defence in an article on the characteristics of G.'s religious experience, which seem to indicate a genuine mystic and a great teacher of mystical theology. Here G.'s Latin is intentionally ambiguous: *Temerarius forsitan videar, qui conor inexperta exponere et de sponsae lectulo, quae illum suavius forsan et secretius collocavit, quam conjectura nostra possit attingere. Quapropter de mysteriis ad mores descendamus.* To translate *inexperta exponere* with Dion as: 'exprimer ces sentiments que je n'ai pas eprouves' or with Miquel: 'exposer des experiences que je n'ai pas faites' is an unwarranted clarification of G.'s intentional ambiguity. Gilbert writes cautiously, twice adding 'perhaps' [*forsitan . . . forsan*]; his *inexperta exponere* need not imply his own lack of experience but could reflect the general lack of such experience or the particular inexperience of his one correspondent; finally he is being as discreet as his master, Bernard, who wrote, in SC 85: 'Now someone may perhaps ask me what it is like to enjoy the Word. I shall answer him: seek out rather someone who has had experience and ask him. For if it has been given to me, even to such as me, to have that experience, do you think that I could express the inexpressible?' After discussing mysteries of the spiritual life, *de mysteriis,* for seven paragraphs, G. descends to some practical observations on the ascetical life, *ad mores.*

SERMON 3
THE INITIATIVE

Importunate love initiates the quest through the city of God. 1. It is grievous to seek and not find. 2. The bride laments the Bridegroom's absence. 3. Brooking no delay, she goes searching herself. 4. Though he is everywhere, she rises not like the prodigal but like Mary going into the hill country. 5. Open to all is his mercy, not his delights, but love follows him everywhere.

I HAVE SOUGHT HIM BUT I HAVE NOT FOUND HIM. I WILL ARISE AND GO ABOUT THE CITY; I WILL SEEK HIM THROUGH THE STREETS AND THE SQUARES*

Sg 3:1-2.

The Bridegroom is not always wont to meet the desires of the soul which seeks him, either at the time or in the measure requested. 'I have sought him' she says, 'but 'I have not found him'. 'I have sought him' is a gracious statement, but 'I have not found him is grievous. How could it not be grievous and unbearable to one who seeks and loves as she does? No soul is denied her heart's desire without anxiety, but her distress is the more acute if, on the crest of hope and on the very verge of success, she is cheated. How much more is she distressed who is pierced by hunger for an interior sweetness once tasted and now lost! One may well believe that in proportion to the amount of sweetness recalled in retrospect in the heart, with so much sharper a spur is the lover's spirit goaded towards the quest. In brief, the depth of one's love tells the depth of one's grief when one fails in the quest. If anyone has ever personally experienced such a feeling of love or of longing, by projecting his own experience he can appreciate with what a petulant heart the bride blurted out: 'I have not found him'.

Nowhere is there consolation, nowhere relief, but everywhere I found tribulation and sorrow, while I failed to find him whom I love ardently and seek relentlessly. You have treated me, I do not say as your foe but as a stranger to you and 'I have become a burden to myself'.* A burden indeed, since I am weary of life and of the light of day, because 'even the very light of my eyes is not with me'. Where will consolation exist without, if in your absence all is disturbance within me? 'My heart is confounded, my strength has abandoned me and even the very light of my eye is not with me'.* These three blessings have vanished with you: power, truth, and identity. For how was power present on a bed of grief, or the light of truth in the night, or the 'self-same' in division and separation? To me now applies Jeremiah's reproach: 'How long will you stray, my wayward daughter'?* Cain, too, after he left the face of the Lord, became a wanderer and a fugitive.* Not in Cain's way am I a wanderer and a fugitive, for I am in pursuit rather than in flight and, to be frank, flight applies rather to you. Or am I not a wanderer when I pass from the confines of my little bed to the breadth of the city, running through the squares and streets, past the watchmen? 'He who clings to the Lord is one spirit with him'.* Union is sweet and so separation is bitter.

2. How has this identity been dissolved, this union sundered, so that I have returned to myself diminished by half? For I did not wholly depart from you. Though in yearning I am swept towards you, I am kept from your presence. Whatever solace I have in my yearning is wholly hidden and swallowed up by the ordeal of waiting. How is it all solace is not hidden as long as you hide your face from me? As Hosea says: 'Consolation is hidden from my eyes'*,

Jb 7:20.

Ps 37:11.

Jr 31:22.
Gn 4:16.

1 Co 6:17.

Hos 13:14-15.

because division has been caused among my beloved.'[1] But from me consolation is hidden, because
to me this union had been granted. Of course you
need none of my goods,* for my goods are your   *Ps 15:2.*
gifts. Therefore desolation overwhelms me as long as
I happen to be separated from you. You are my
courage, you are the light of my eyes, you are my
very self, you are my all. As the psalmist says: 'my
flesh and my heart have failed me',* so that neither   *Ps 72:26.*
carnal affection nor the feeling of my heart breathes
any longer in me; but let God be the God of my
heart, and let him be my portion for ever. If I lose
this portion I shall be left empty and barren like
parched soil and a broken jar.

You who are inebriated lift up, lift up one who
thirsts and pour a portion of your plenty into my
empty jar.* Why be so sparing with that torrent of   *See T 6:4.*
your abundance? Woe is me! How swiftly your
torrent sweeps through our valleys!* It passes like a   *Jb 6:15.*
flash flood, but its shared delights draw me in their
wake into endless longing. Delights depart but they
leave longing behind. Delights are fugitives but longing is a rack-master. The sweeter the draft once
tasted, the more tantalizing the ordeal of delay. Will
it seem so delightful to you, O Lord, to torment a
pitiful soul with such delay and to laugh at the
torments of one who loves you and seeks you? If
majesty sets you apart, let mercy make you stoop
down. If you do not yield yourself to your beloved's
affection, at least take pity on her affliction. Af-
flicted am I and exceedingly humbled; from the
anguish of my heart I moan within myself, 'I have
not found him'.* Where now is the abundance of   *Ps 37:9.*
your heart's pity and compassion? Long, and too
long, have they failed to flow over me. Your beloved
pours herself out in sorrow with longing for you, an
absentee, and do you refuse to pour yourself out?

When Joseph felt compassion for his brothers who
had served him so badly, he could not contain himself; moved to the depth he graciously revealed his
identity.* Indeed the devotion of a bridegroom   *Gn 45:1-3.*
usually manifests a more tender affection than the

devotion of a brother. You are more to me than a
Joseph, for you are my brother and my bridegroom.

Sg 8:1.

'Who will restore you to me as my brother'?* I ex-
pend myself wholly in the quest for you, Brother and
Bridegroom, and do you keep me in suspense? Alas,
will you be less in love because you are greater in
majesty? Love and humility have more in common
than love and majesty. For a moment forget your
majesty that you may remember your mercy. All
my longing is for you in your absence. Why is it not
in your presence? Why is my moaning hidden from
you when it is wholly for you? You feign not to hear,
you put me off and turn your face from me, so that I

Ps 29:8.

am thrown into confusion.* Therefore I complain
and lament and cry out: 'I have not found him.'

3.   Happy will be my state when I am allowed to
say: 'My Beloved is mine and I am his'. Really, I do
belong to my Beloved but he is not yet 'turned

Sg 2:16; 7:10.

towards me'.* Bitter indeed is change for a lover!
Therefore in turn I change my cry: 'I have not found
him'. 'All things have their hour and all things under
the sun hurry past in their places'. When will it happen that all things become as fixed as the sun, and
that instead of being as changeable as the moon, they
stop in eternity and do not run by in time? But
now all things have their time and perhaps eternity
itself has its own time, for we speak of eternal periods
of time. The things of eternity then are eternal in
themselves but for us they have been prepared at their
proper time. All things have their proper time; there
is a time for embracing and a time for refraining

Qo 3:1-8.

from embraces.* What time then will be more suitable for embracing than night? Indeed what place
will be more suitable for embracing than the little
bed, what time more suitable than night? In peace is
your place and likewise your time of repose, and my
little bed of peace I have prepared for you in my
heart. Let my Beloved come, let my delight come
and rest in his bed. Perhaps according to your
appointment book you keep me waiting; but impatient love draws no comfort from an appointment
book! I know that comfort is kept in store to be

given me in due time but love complains of the
snail's pace of fleeting time. You keep me waiting;
for my part I can bear it no longer but 'will arise and
go about the city'.*   *Sg 3:2.*
I scorn my little bed and
abandon the first half of my cry, that I may be
swept forward to what is more perfect.

4. For although I am a bride and perfect within
the narrow limit of our human condition, I consider
that I have received only a beginning as I anticipate
what is to come: 'I will arise and go about the city,
I will seek him through the streets and the squares'.[2]
Good Jesus, why is it that you are not found in
some places, when faith says you are everywhere?
There are indeed many halls in your Father's house,*   *Jn 14:2.*
but do you abandon some when you pass to others,
you who are infinite and unbounded by space? Everywhere in your creation you are present whole and
entire, creating and conserving; but no creature can
express your infinity though every creature can hint
imperfectly at your power. You are present everywhere whole and entire by your existence, but not
equally in each and every creature by your causality.
Although you act everywhere of yourself whole and
entire, you may not activate the fullness of your
power everywhere; indeed you do so nowhere. Yes,
with one and the same excellence you perform the
least actions on the least occasions and greater
actions on great occasions. Therefore although your
excellence acts everywhere whole and entire, it is
nowhere wholly exhausted, for you are able at will
to do greater things; your excellence is not given its
full expression, because images cannot convey reality
in its entirety.

All things then exhibit you to me for my knowledge, but not everything can move me inwardly to
devotion. Everywhere I stumble upon you, but not
everywhere am I touched to the heart![3] Everywhere
the beauty, value and harmony of the universe
thrusts you upon my attention, but as the Word
which is Wisdom, not as the Word which is Salvation.
The Word which is wisdom and salvation, that is,
Christ Jesus, exists only in the city of our God, upon

his holy mountain. Therefore 'I will arise and go
about the city'. 'Awake you who sleep', says Paul,
'arise from the dead and Christ will shine upon

Eph 5:14.

you'.* For my part I will arise not from dead works,
not from evil works, but from good to better, from
morals to mysteries, from mysteries to revelations,
from visions to delights. 'I will arise and go about'
that city of which it is said, 'Great is the Lord and
worthy of all praise in the city of our God, upon his

Ps 47:2.
Lk 1:39.

holy mountain'.* Just so must one arise who wishes
to go up into the hill country with Mary.* Even the
prodigal son, coming to his senses, resolves: 'I will

Lk 15:18ff.

arise and go to my father'.* Prudently he says 'I will
arise', as he intends to go to the Father who is in
heaven. But the hope he nourished in his breast was
too thin and emaciated, for he intended to ask his
father to be treated as a hired hand. His decision, a
fair estimate of his deserts, was an excessively low
and unjust estimate of the bounty of his father's
mercy. Herein he showed the marks of a spirit really
starved and broken by hunger when he resolved: 'I
will say to him: "Father, treat me as one of your
hired hands".' He could not make his famished and
wasted hope extend to anything greater. 'I will arise',
he says, 'and go to my father'. The lad is moved by
anxiety not to find, but only to influence, his father.
One who is a bride and assured of favor asks only for
the presence of the Beloved. 'I will arise', she says,
'and go about the city and seek him whom my soul
loves', thinking it enough to find him.

5.   Consider whether this difference cannot be observed in comparing these texts: that the Father's for-
giveness is available to all, waiting for all, but that his
delights are fleeting and hidden, and haunt secret shel-
ters.[4] Hence the son says 'I will arise and go', but the
bride says: 'I will arise and seek'. Though the Father
runs to meet his repentant son, the Bridegroom withdraws from his beloved. Mercy pours itself out more
freely, delight more sparingly. Yet the same resolution
proposed by both the son and the bride, 'I will arise', is
not inconsistent. Paul does not allow you to seek the

Col 3:1.

things which are above, unless you have first arisen.*

You cannot have any taste for the things which are above unless you have first sought them. For what is it to find those good things which are above but to relish them fully by some savor of sweetness and experience? Therefore the bride scans, and scrutinizes everything that somewhere she may savor what she loves. 'I will arise,' she says, 'and go about the city, through the streets and the squares I will seek him whom my soul loves.' Holy love promotes much personal initiative. For how much do you think she loved when she presumed so much? 'I will arise', she says, 'and go about the city'.

No hypocrite, Lord, will come into your sight. Adam hid himself after he lost the hardihood of a good conscience* and grieved that he was detected when he ought rather to have been the detective. *Gn 3:8.* A false lover flees from your sight, but a true bride endowed with the gift of charity pursues you even when you take flight. Where will you go, good Jesus, from the face of passionate desire? If you mount into heaven, her desire is there; if you go down to the depths, desire is present. Everywhere, like an anxious sleuth,[5] she follows you ranging throughout all your creation step by step. What she possesses by faith she tries to transform into affection and to match by her devotion your amazing Majesty. She applies all the Gospel records to the kindling of her love, that where she gathers your truth, there she may experience your power, your very self, her Bridegroom, Christ Jesus, you who live and reign for ever and ever. Amen.[6]

NOTES TO SERMON THREE

1.   G: *quia facta est inter dilectos divisio;* Vulg.: *Quia ipse inter fratres dividet.*

2.   G. begins here his remarkable development of *circuitus,* the soul's spiritual pilgrimage.

3.   ' . . . *non ubique compungor.* I do not everywhere feel compunction;' See Lam. p. 193, nn. 151-155, and index under 'compunction'.

4.   The sentence begins with *vide,* second person singular, the only clue given of his audience.

5.   *curiosa scrutatrix:* see Lam p. 184, nn. 90, 92.

6.   Lam p. 180, n. 64.

SERMON 4.
ROAMING THE CITY OF GOD

*Love tracks the Beloved through his planned
city. 1. She roams in familiar spiritual haunts.
2. For the progress of the believing soul,
reason mediates between faith and understanding. 3. The lover learns of God's creation,
conservation, providence and concurrence;
4–6. the lover learns with the wise and praises
with the saints the action of God in salvation
history; 7. finds here threefold matter for contemplation and the difference between sur-
rounding* (circuitus) *and embracing* (com-
plexus). *8. The wheel of desire stops only with
the Beloved. 9. What becomes of the search*
(circuitus) *in the company of the angels in
heaven?*

I WILL ARISE AND GO ABOUT THE CITY,
THROUGH THE STREETS AND THE SQUARES
I WILL SEEK HIM WHOM MY SOUL LOVES*[1]   *Sg 3:2.*

T his circuit of the city is not the tour of
a gadabout but the quest of a lover. If
the bride wanders in making this circuit,
still she does not stray, she does not
leave the boundaries of the city nor the haunts
where her Beloved is wont to walk. In making her
rounds she walks, walks interiorly through the
streets and squares of the city. 'In these streets
Wisdom manifests himself with merriment' and 'in
the squares he breaks into song'.*   *Ws 6:17.*

73

these thoroughfares, because she knows where she encounters her Beloved more frequently. 'In my quest', she says, 'I will go about the streets and squares'. Many a time, O happy soul, you make your rounds; the approach is familiar and every detail of the city is known to you: its highways and byways, back lanes and broad squares. 'The king led you into his wine cellar'.* Did he not also lead you into all other more secret hiding-places? To you everything is unlocked and accessible,[2] and from practice you feel ready for this happy journey. Not with reluctance then, but with confidence, she says: 'I will go about the city'.

Sg 2:4.

How much do you suppose it consoles her, brothers, to retrace all the while and repeatedly tread in the footprints where the feet of her Beloved used to stand? The places where we have experienced some blessing somehow imprint that blessing more vividly on our memory, paint it in detail before our mind's eye, and what we once experienced there we expect a second time. Those places, in my view, are not physical but spiritual haunts conducive to the spiritual exercise of the soul. Let us assume then that her roaming occurs in spiritual haunts.[3]

2. This progress is one either of recall or of inquiry. For in a way one progresses who either recollects what he knows or from what he knows deduces something hitherto unknown. He somehow progresses who recalls what he knows or detects something new. It is progress of a kind, when what we already hold by faith and understanding we review systematically. It is progress of a kind, when from truths we already hold we advance and enter into deeper mysteries. The former is progress of delight, the latter of reason. The former is more loving, the latter more subtle. Though the former seems more appropriate to the bride, still we shall deprive her of neither. For whether she retraces what is already known through discovery or probes into the unknown, in all her inquiries she does but seek fresh kindling for the fire of love.

Good is the progress of reason, provided reason

confines itself within the rules of faith and does not stray beyond the bounds of faith, as it ranges 'from faith to faith' or from faith to understanding. Even understanding, should it outstrip faith, gazes on nothing other than what is grasped by faith. In understanding there is not greater certainty than in faith but greater clarity. Neither admits error or uncertainty. Where error or uncertainty exists, understanding does not exist; where uncertainty exists, there is no faith. But if faith seems capable of admitting error, it is not the true or the catholic faith but a mistaken credulity. If I may speak in metaphor, faith embraces and clings to unbending truth; understanding gazes upon truth unveiled and naked; reason attempts to remove the veils. Reason, mediating between faith and understanding, stands erect by faith but stretches upwards on tiptoe to understanding.

Reason desires something more than to believe. What more? To behold. It is one thing to believe and another to behold; yet reason does not strive to behold anything other than what it conceives by faith. And if reason be not yet able to see clearly, still by some suitable speculations reason attempts to construct logically what it has already accepted on the firm foundation of faith. Reason makes an effort beyond faith but by faith is supported and by faith restrained; in the first instance the mind is devout, in the second prudent, in the third sober, for if you will pardon the rhyme, faith enfolds, reason upholds, understanding beholds. Good is this journey, wherein the mind advances step by step under the guidance of reason without straying from the faith, because guided by faith and harnessed to faith. But the mind obviously strays if it does not submit everything to the scrutiny of faith and rein in the quick gallop of reason to the steady gait of faith.

Good is the journey when by proceeding from faith to faith the justice of God is revealed.* Good is the journey when one is transformed from splendor to splendor as if by the Spirit of the Lord.* Good is the journey when forgetting what lies behind, one presses on to what lies ahead in the hope of somehow

Rm 1:17. On par. 2, see Bernard Csi V:ii:4-5; CF 37:144-145.

2 Co 3:18.

Ph 3:12-13.
See Bernard, Csi
V:ii:4-5; CF 37:
141-142.

reaching one's goal.* Good assuredly is the journey
not only whenever new and more hidden truths are
grasped but also when truths already grasped are
unfolded with an affection ever new and ever fresh,
not only when one covers new ground but also when
frequently one retraces ground already covered.
Delightful then is the journey, one not unknown to
the bride for she says confidently: 'I will rise and go
about the city'.

3. What city can be suggested more appropriate
than the city in this text: 'Glorious things have been
told of you, O city of God'?*[4] The created universe,
of course, can aptly be called the city of God, for by
him was it founded and by him was it set in array.
Glorious obviously is this city both in its beauty and
in its harmony. Less glorious it may seem[5] in the
disorderly conduct which derives from the freedom
of wicked minds, as far as their conduct is concerned;
nor is it any thanks to their conduct that they do
not elude the plan of God's providence, though his
plan be far from their intention. They alone are
really glorious, however, who eagerly follow the
divine pattern, keen to preserve intact the grace of
their original state or to mend it if ever it is rent.
These latter are made glorious in two ways: by a
natural state shared with others and by a voluntary
conformity not shared by others, to the will of God
who orders and directs all things.

Ps 86:3.

The created universe then is called the city of
God, since it is governed by the laws of his economy.
He bestows on each and every creature the fair form
of existence in its own genus, its effectiveness in
practice, its rightful place in due order, that each
may be beautiful in itself, not superfluous as part of
the whole, and neither out of joint nor at odds in
relation to others. For whether a creature is moved
by the impulse of nature of by the free thrust of its
own choice or by the prompting of divine grace, or
whether by each of these causes separately or by all
of them together, every creature receives its form
and its impulse from the divine efficiency invisibly
acting within, yes, its form and, as it were, the law

of its order and the impulse of its action. For not
only the innate faculty of any action but also
the action of any faculty is granted by God, so that
both alike, the power to act and the activation of the
power, come from God. Yet an action which proceeds from an evil intention depends on him for the
act's existence but not for its own evil. God is not
responsible for the fact that the action is directed to
a disorderly end, but God is responsible for the fact
that disorder itself is restored to order by a really
amazing design.

4. Consider how the selling of Joseph, the descent
into Egypt, the exodus and Pharoah's pursuit, the
drowning of his army and the deliverance of Israel
illustrate the mysteries of Christ's incarnation and
passion and of our deliverance. In many places with
application[6] you will find similar parallels. The
delinquencies of old then could only serve to illustrate
new mysteries, if divine Providence were working
through them in a hidden plan. For those events of
old did not so happen by chance and so much without purpose that subsequently more recent mysteries were made to accord with them by a skilled
planner, a careful observer; but rather the former
were devised not by any human design but by God's
disposition, to bring out the meaning of the latter;
the latter were not made to harmonize with the
former. Why was the Lord delivered up to his passion
particularly at that time? Why was he subjected to
that kind of death at that hour and on that day?
Who would either say these events have no symbolic
meaning or suppose them fortuitous? On the very
day of the week that man was created, he was
redeemed; at the very hour he was sentenced, he was
granted pardon. By a tree death made its entrance
and by a tree life was restored.

Yet somebody actually claims that these parallels
are not the result of divine economy but of human
management. As evidence, Sir, you have the season
of the paschal lamb and you have the spotless victim;
you have the hour of the Israelites' deliverance from
Egypt and you have the grace of your deliverance

from the errors and vanity of the world and from
your corrupt nature; yet do you believe that this
simply happened, [it happened] not by God's dispensation but by the intervention of a Jew quite unaware
of the import of his actions? This close concurrence
of evidence concerning the tree of the cross, the time,
the hour, the day and the other circumstances which
can be carefully recorded, do you, I ask, ascribe to
the folly of the Jews and not to the wisdom of God?
By that remedy of the cross, which thoroughly heals
that folly and converges in one pattern of evidence
with the mysteries of old, mere chance and human
intuition are excluded as explanations but not a
divine design. In the prophecy of Isaiah also you will
find this said to Hezekiah: 'All these things have

Is 39:6. been given into the hands of the Chaldaeans'.* By the
word 'given', the text shows that they were not only
prophetically foretold but also directed as if by a
court of justice.

In the light of these and similar passages here and
there throughout Scripture, who will harbor any
doubt that divine power and wisdom alike, by their
just laws, do not indeed inspire but rather counter-
balance the depraved wills of rational creatures? If
that is so, much less can anyone doubt that the
actions of other living creatures, which are led by
natural instinct and determined only by the judgement of their senses or imagination, not by the free
choice of reason, are in no way exempt from the
divine disposition. To sum up, the essence of all
things which places them in this or that class of being,
their existence which gives them being and their
usefulness which makes them efficient causes, are
moved and changed and restrained by the eternal and
unchangeable ordinances and decrees of a most just,
most powerful, most wise governor, who rules the
whole of creation with an undeviating justice, like the
most orderly and the best planned of cities.

5. Is the city through which the bride proposes
to journey this whole created universe? The wise
men of this world visited the natural phenomena of
the universe and discerned the wisdom of God at

work in his masterpiece. At work, I say, but not that work of which we read: 'God, our king from of old, has completed his saving work in the midst of the earth'.* They recognized the craftsman in this work but gave him neither glory nor thanks.[7]

Ps 73:12.

The believing soul records and reviews all things to the praise of God and calls on every creature to glorify him, in order to arouse herself to gratitude and be spurred to love God by contemplation of the universe. Solomon visited and discussed all things, from the cedar of Lebanon to the hyssop.* In Ecclesiastes, he visited the elements and, after treating of their revolution, turned his consideration to human actions, thus passing from the fleeting vanity of things to the truth which endures. Job visited, or rather was conducted by the Lord around, the foundations of the earth, through its measure, plumb-line and supports, its cornerstones, the stars of morning and the jubilation of God's sons: through the gates of the sea, its womb, the cloud in which it was wrapped as in the swaddlingclothes of infancy; through boundaries, bars and gates, through the rising of early morn, the place of dawn and through other fixed phenomena of the created universe.*

1 K 4:23.

Jb 38:4-12.

It took time to enumerate all his creatures, but all are calculated to produce admiration of their Creator in one who gazes on the universe soberly and love in one who reflects upon it devoutly. This universe is exhibited without exception to all endowed with reason and it proclaims the majesty of its Creator by the fair form of its beauty. Yet more beautiful still, beneath their fair covering, are the hidden mysteries of our salvation and the manifold gifts of spiritual graces.

6. Again at the end of the Book of Psalms, after summoning every creature to praise God. David also adds: 'Sing to the Lord a new song, let his praise resound in the assembly of the saints'.* Truly a new song, for its theme never grows old and its pleasure never cloys. Love makes it ever fresh, repetition fresher still. This song is truly new for it renews the spirits of mankind for eternal beatitude. Again we

Ps 149:1,
Lam 6, n. 6.

Is 43:18-19.

read: 'Do not remember former things, look not upon the things of old; for I also make things new'.* Rightly are they new, in no way included in the laws of nature current from days of old. 'Let his praise resound in the assembly of the saints', yes, by virtue of their excellence, not so much by a dispensation of justice but by the free gift and blessing of holiness.

'Let his praise resound in the assembly of the saints', because the action of the saints so manifests his praise that their affection ministers to his praise. For saints surpass others in welcoming the gifts of grace, in deep feelings of devotion and in rendering due thanks. Therefore by a special prerogative God is praised in the assembly of the saints, while outside the assembly God is praised by the unintelligent and mute service of creatures and by the hollow service of mankind. In unintelligent things praise is limited by their nature; in men not born to new life, praise is limited to their knowledge. But in neither does love exist. In the former, love of their Creator is non-existent, in the latter love is unsanctified. 'Let his praise resound in the assembly of the saints.' For how the order of nature exists in accord with its essence, how the order of grace exists without disharmony or disorder, how the pursuit of destiny leads to happiness, this whole universe the saint researches and weighs in proportion to his gifts, that thereby he may gain some adequate notion of the powers of his Maker, set out to imitate him, and be swept towards love for him.

7. This then is the spiritual city, this is the assembly of the saints, through which the bride makes bold to say she will journey. O God of goodness, what valuable reflections are here in abundance! For who can adequately appreciate how fair and how numerous are the splendors which exist everywhere in mysteries, in models, in miracles? Mysteries refer to salvation, models refer to conduct, miracles refer to witness. But what happens when the mind rises from mystery and from morality to marvel at the eternal reward for temporal merits? What waves of joy meet the outpouring of our longing! 'Children of

men, how long are you to love what is empty and
seek what is false'?* Why turn your spirit to strange
allurements, why seek in labor for elusive delights?
The source of joy you have at hand in the mysteries
of our faith, stored in the memory, fruitful for meditation, unfailing for your nourishment, abundant for
your satisfaction.

Ps 4:3. See Lam 183, n. 84.

Children of men or rather children of the Most
High, sons of a religious order whose footsteps wear
away the threshold of regular discipline,[8] why
thirst with parched lips for muddied waters and
disdain the waters of heaven? Why admit into your
mind thoughts to which you do not commit your
hand? Why handle assiduously in your mind what
you utterly disdain to touch? You know from frequent experience that the recall of all this empty
parade of remembered wantonness is wont to end
abruptly in remorse. As Job suggests, this is shameful to reveal and painful to conceal.* Change then
the subject of your meditations but safeguard your
earnestness. How disgraceful it is that your enthusiasm should be diminished when its object is
changed for the better!

Jb 6:20. See Lam 183, n. 83.

But I do say this: as you once exposed your
spirit to the alluring considerations of defiling wantonness, so now expose your spirit to the fruitful
quest for the beauty of truth. 'Surround Sion' says
the psalmist 'and embrace her'.* Surround her in
meditation, embrace her in love. Embrace her that
your grasp of her may be complete and your
caress intimate. More seems to be implied by 'embrace' than by 'surround'; 'embrace' takes in the
whole all at once, 'surround' passes on successively
from part to part. Yet 'surround' seems superior in
this respect: that we make no distinctions and
notice no difference when we 'embrace'; whereas
when we 'surround' we examine each part separately.
'To embrace' is to be content with the whole; 'to
surround' is to take each part individually.

Ps 47:13, see Lam 184, n. 87.

8. The spirit which hungers and thirsts, finding
itself unsatisfied by a few blessings, is always borne
on towards the remainder. The spirit is whirled in a

kind of circle, stretched on the wheel of its spinning desires, until hunger for love is sated with blessings and manages to stop its flight in a love wherein no limit is found. Since all things created are finite by their very nature, the mind in its quest passes by all of them, unable to rest wherever it discovers the finite. He alone is rest for the lover and refreshment, who is the end of all things and who exists without end. Accordingly, the bride in her quest passes by all other things to arrive at him: 'I will arise', she says, 'and go about the city'. I will go about seeking in all things him whom I love but finding him nowhere. 'His invisible attributes are visible to the eye of reason in the things he has made.'*

Rm 1:20.

Yet no creature, however excellent it may be and however closely it may imitate him, fully instructs me by its evidence or inflames me by its service. For the service of his creatures in portraying their Creator is found to be as dull, slow and ineffectual as statues are known to be inferior to the original. Therefore 'I will go about the city', approaching everything, passing everything by: approaching them as far as each in its own way portrays his likeness; passing them by when they fall short of perfection. 'I will go about the city', everywhere tasting refreshment only to experience distaste. For how am I not refreshed by what bears some pledge, shows some sign, recalls some memory, suggests some knowledge of my love? But again how do I not suffer disappointment, as I reflect that I am being cozened with an image, delayed by a shadow and that I do not possess the naked and simple reality? 'I will go about the city', because in its wide expanse, so fair, I am everywhere encouraged but nowhere renewed.

9. Making my rounds will not weary me until a fuller approach is opened to me, that I may enter into the sanctuary of God and gain understanding of his ultimate mysteries. Then our journey comes to an end, when we shall be replenished with the blessings of your house, O Lord, when in your ultimate mysteries I shall understand you who are first and last, the beginning and the end.* O what a journey

Rv 21:6.

will be there, hastening from yourself to yourself, ever going and returning: going by desire, returning in delight, while your presence ever satisfies what our experience desires, so that the mind which holds and beholds you is at once intent upon you by attraction and content with you by satisfaction.

So those 'winged spirits covered with eyes', are said to be 'in the centre and around God's throne'.* *Rv 4:26.* 'In the centre', because they are led into the inmost circle of their desires; 'on the circumference' because they are drawn into the same circle by an ever quickening desire. 'In the centre' because their desire is already fulfilled; 'on the circumference' because they are unable to comprehend its totality. They have been welcomed 'into the center' by grace; they have been kept 'on the circumference' by their distinct nature. They are 'in the centre' because they are united by contemplation and they are 'on the circumference' because they are distinguished by comparison. For what is your throne but that unapproachable light of which the apostle speaks, in which God dwells?* However, no matter how many *1 Tm 6:16.* eyes those blessed spirits may have, your light both illumines them that they may see to the limit of their vision, and yet your light surpasses them lest their vision encompass you entirely.

Oh what broad vistas have the lookouts there! What sweeping horizons have the plazas in that infinity of light! How well linked and articulated, how extensive are the streets in that simplicity, that charity and that eternity! 'Those byways are byways of beauty and those paths are paths of peace'.* No *Ws 3:17.* one loses his way or struggles in vain on those paths. There from every direction the Bridegroom approaches, presents himself, as it were, with glad countenance and melts into the heart of his beloved, that for the future he need not be sought, Jesus Christ, who lives and reigns for ever and ever. Amen.[9]

NOTES TO SERMON FOUR

1.   The singular *vide*, par. 4, suggests a treatise adapted to his audience of *fratres*, par. 1, and *alumni religionis*, par. 7. For this spiritual pilgrimage of the soul within the cloister, G. avoids the wealth of scriptural and historical allusions in the ambiguous words 'pilgrim' and 'pilgrimage' in favor of his text and the scriptural riches of the equally ambiguous *circuitus* and *circuibo*. See Jean Leclercq, *'Aux sources de la spiritualite occidentale'* (Paris: Cerf, 1964) 35-90, especially 78-85; *'Le pelerinage interieur';* and his *'Vocabulaire Monastique',* SAn 48 (1961) 164, *peregrinatio.* See also L. Braceland, 'Spiritual Pilgrimage', in *Cistercian Studies,* 12 (1977).

2.   Reading *pervia* with Migne, rather than *brevia* with Mab.

3.   Lam, 177, n. 43; 184, n. 88.

4.   Four key words in par. 3, appear in Augustine: *motus* frequently in the *Confessions; modus, species, ordo* occur together in *De Civitate Dei;* CCSL Pars XIV, 1 (Turnholt: Brepols, 1955) V:11 p. 142, lines 10-11; on these three words, see Gilson, *The Christian Philosophy of St. Augustine,* tr. Lynch (London; Gollancz, 1961) 180-182.

5.   Reading *minus* rather than *nimis.*

6.   Mab. omits *diligens;* see Dt 17:4; Lam 180 n. 62.

7.   Rm 1:21; perhaps an allusion to Lucretius, *De Rerum Natura.*

8.   See Lam 170, nn. 3, 4; for the benedictine expression here, see also G. S 35:7; G. speaks of the round of regular observance in S 23:3, alludes here and there to particular observances, and presents the monastic day from vigils to nightfall in S 23:3. See also S 43:8.

9.   On par. 8-9, de Lubac impishly remarks in *Exegese* 1:595, n. 9, 'Ce jour-la au moins, Gilbert avait herite de l'inspiration de Bernard'.

SERMON 5,
SEEK WITH WISDOM AND AFFECTION

*Love seeks everywhere with wise freedom and
pure affection. 1. The word of the Beloved is a
delightful banquet. 2-3. Christ cannot be found
in Jewish interpretations and pagan teaching;
4-5, he can be found in the way of the
commandments and of the counsels; 6. he is
found in the active and contemplative life,
especially among Cistercians; 7. he is found in
desolation and consolation. 8. But note the
distinction between worldly and godly wisdom; 9. the former frequents lawcourts. 10. The
name of Jesus is found on men's lips but rarely
in their hearts.*

THROUGH THE STREETS AND SQUARES I WILL
SEEK HIM WHOM MY SOUL LOVES.*

*Sg 3:2;
G. addresses one
person
throughout.*

Yesterday's sermon travelled a long way in
following the bride's progress. Thanks
be to you, Lord Jesus Christ, for making
your sayings so sweet to my palate,[1]
surpassing honey in my mouth. So one mouthful,
once tasted, scarcely leaves the tongue to be replaced
by another. Slowly each morsel is masticated, or if it
is swallowed whole, with a kind of gentle eructation
it returns for rumination.[2] All this could have been
said trippingly on the tongue but the flavor of the
subject matter titillates a gourmet's palate, creates an
appetite for itself, and does not readily vanish once
placed on the table for discussion. Similarly when a

85

nurse has broken off a crust and has with some vigorous chewing thoroughly masticated it for an infant's nourishment, sometimes she keeps it on her tongue, relishing the flavor of its taste. So breaking up the solid food of this Canticle for others if need be, we too cannot squander the sweetness once tasted but we so minister to another's needs as partially to satisfy our own wants.

Just when I think the sermon ended and brought to a satisfactory conclusion, the banquet of the word with an aroma not to be denied makes my mouth water and as memory reopens a cupboard full of delicacies another tray is served for discussion. But why not? Why not shake most frequently that fig tree whose fruit is never fully shaken off? Why be surprised if that tree is more often stripped which is made more fruitful by plucking its fruit, when it seems to vie with the hand of the picker and to surpass his greed by its own fruitfulness? Not such as the fig tree the Lord Jesus cursed, for finding no fruit on it he made what was fruitless everlastingly barren.*

Mk 11:13-14.
See Virgil,
Aeneid, 6:136-44,
201-11, the
golden bough.

2. See how the faith of Christ made barren the traditions of the Jews and the tenets of the philosophers. See how faith dried up the rivers of Egypt! One cannot find in their doctrines and interpretations the fruit of which one reads in the psalm: 'Our soil will yield its fruit'.* Christ cannot be found in their streets and squares. Already he has escaped from your bonds, O Jews, already he left his house, abandoned his heritage.* According to Isaiah, you have become 'like a shanty in à melon-patch, like a city laid waste'.* Even of your squares he nonetheless adds 'truth stumbles in the squares'.* Concerning the philosophers of the Gentiles, Paul says they imprisoned the truth in falsehood.* Does it not seem appropriate to you to take the streets to mean Israel according to the flesh, since they came of the one stock of Abraham and were fitted and compressed into one narrow rite, bound by one law? But the wise men of the Gentiles are rightly symbolized

Ps 83:13; see
de Lubac, Exegese
2:144.

Jr 12:7.

Is 1:8.

Is 59:14.

Rm 1:18, 25.

by the squares, because in their unbridled liberty and
licence they strayed from the path of truth, and
concerning the majesty of God expressed opinions
no less discordant with his dignity than repugnant to
his truth. The Jews, through lack of understanding,
concentrating on the uniqueness of the divine nature, were unable to extend the growth of their faith
to include the persons of the Son and the Holy
Spirit. The philosophers of the Gentiles, wandering
over the plain and restrained by no frontier of divine
teaching, adopted gods many in nature and number-
less in person; each held views at variance with his
fellows and all together held opinions empty and
vain.

3. But what soul now seeks the Bridegroom in
their streets or squares? If any there be, she is a concubine or an adulteress. The concubine shares only a
temporary roof with a bridegroom; the adulteress, a
roof she betrays. Why should anyone knock there,
where dwells not chaste wisdom but that of an alien
or a harlot? Such a creature is sketched for you in
the book of Proverbs: 'coming to meet a silly youth
when he crosses the square near the corner at twilight
and dead of night, a woman in harlot's guise, decked
out to hunt souls, garrulous and homeless; now on
the highway, now in the square, now at some corner
she waits in ambush'.* I am wary of such a square, in   *Pr 7:7.*
which a woman so sly and shifty devises the ambush
of her charms for a silly youth. For something dark,
distorted and counterfeit is conveyed to me by the
night, the corner and the harlot's disguise.

I suspect, or at least disdain, any doctrine which
makes no mention of Christ, which neither renews
me by his sacraments nor teaches me by his precepts
nor enkindles me with his promises. Now the Jews do
indeed have him in their scrolls but not in their interpretation. For a veil still exists over their minds
rather than over their law. Nor can the veil be removed except when they turn to the Lord. Both in
their beliefs about God and in their morals for men,
I hold suspect the licence of the one, the narrowness
of the other and the stubbornness of both. I little like

the multiplicity which the one posits in the divine
nature, the singularity which the other asserts and the
blindness of both. So I would not attribute to the
bride any search for her Beloved in their streets and
squares. Let us assign other streets, other squares to
her whom Christ has betrothed to himself in faith
and in truth.

4. Of course there are two ways of life among
the faithful. Some follow the broad way, others
pledge themselves to a very strict discipline. For
although it is written: 'Narrow is the way which
leads to life,* in the same genus are two species, and
in comparison with the narrower way another is
regarded as broader. Or do you not recognize the
breadth of the commandment where no one is
obliged to perfection, but the opportunity to remain
in a lower degree is conceded not only to weakness of
health but also to weakness of will? Thanks be to
you, Lord Jesus Christ, because you offer us opportunities for salvation and because you propose the
counsels to the vigorous and energetic in such a way
that you also provide a remedy for the sick and dispense a stimulant for the slothful.[3] Your holy city
Jerusalem has not only streets for those who live
austerely but also squares for those who love the
more lowly and level plains. In every way of life and
in every order, she who is the bride seeks traces of
the one she chastely loves so that from each of them
she may draw a model for her action and fuel for her
love. She does not disdain to borrow emblems of excellence even from outsiders who are bound by no
rule of stricter discipline. She considers affection
often more fervent where the order is on a lower
level.

5. What shall we say of those who nowhere seek
opportunities for salvation, but are everywhere cen-
sorious of slackness in the squares and of indiscre-
tion in the streets? In this group are the many who
scrutinize all ways of life and all orders. There they
discover nothing of attraction but plenty for detrac-
tion, falsely maintaining that in some strictness is
excessive, while in others it is nonexistent. Their

Mt 7:14; Lam 11,
nn. 38, 39.

slogan is as pitiable as it is true: 'I have not found
him'.* Certainly your interpretation is distorted   *Sg 3:1.*
when you say: 'Look, Christ is here! No look, he is
there!' But your interpretation is perverse, should
you say: 'No, he is neither here nor there!' The bride
seeks him in both places, both here and there. 'I will
seek through the streets and the squares him whom
my soul loves'. Take the streets to mean strictness,
the squares dispensation. Do not give a pejorative
interpretation to either concerning servants of the
Church. The Church accepts both; in both the bride
seeks Christ. Do not seek Christ in one only. Seek
Christ in both.

Join squares to streets in yourself. Do you ask
how? If you are limited by affliction, either voluntarily undertaken or imposed against your will, let
spiritual joy enlarge your heart within you and already
you have joined squares with streets. Do you not
think that he possesses both, who rejoices because in
distress his heart was opened to joy?* The apostle   *Ps 4:2.*
wished some breadth in the confinement of trials for
those to whom he recommended: 'rejoicing in hope
and patience in distress'.* For breadth refers to hope: *Rm 12:12.*
'having such promises, dearly beloved', he says,
'open wide your hearts'.* Our present circumstances   *2 Co 6:13.*
are straitened, but our hope expands. Our possessions
are limited, our expectations more abundant. Therefore refer these squares to the breadth of our hope.
'Rejoicing in hope' the apostle says. But the prophet
says: 'Your squares shall yet be filled' with choruses
at play.* Do you see how the apostle and the pro-   *Zc 8:5.*
phet agree in what they say about hope and squares?
For to these, both attribute joy.

6. At the same time this further difference
should be noticed: that in streets people dwell for the
amenities of family life, while in squares they gather
to enjoy a holiday.[4] For in the squares are both the
throng and the chorus of those at play and so the
celebration of a happy holiday takes place in the
squares. Good are those squares in which the spirit,
inspired with spry enough agility, exercises itself for
nimble leaps of contemplation. Thus in the squares

the bride seeks her Beloved; released from household chores and disengaged from the dwelling of her
body and abandoning as far as possible her earthly
home, she devotes herself to contemplation with a
joy proportionate to her freedom. Though the time
for dwelling in the streets is longer, time in the
squares is brief indeed but sweeter. In the streets is
the practice and exercise of virtues necessary for us
as long as we linger in the house of this body, whereas
in the squares is some joyous rehearsal of future
beatitude.

Consider now the sequence of the words. The
bride puts first the streets and then the squares.[5] You
have a parallel in the psalm: 'How lovely are your
tabernacles, O Lord of hosts. My soul yearns and
pines for the courts of the Lord'.* Are you surprised at the preciseness of the bride? Follow her
order. Do not assume that you are more prudent or
more prompt than the bride. First exercise yourself
in the work of the virtues, that subsequently you may
climb to a lookout upon the truth. Why try to make
an entrance by way of the exit? With the bride advance through the streets to the squares and with the
psalmist advance, after the tabernacles of the virtues,
to the spacious courts of the truth. Contrariwise, to
reverse the order is perverse.

The narrower the streets, the richer and more free
is the interior leisure of the mind. Why do I say leisure? I would do better to say devotion. A discipline
outwardly strict inwardly expands the soul. Whether
you interpret the squares as freedom or as joyfulness,
where will you find more spacious squares than in
this Order of ours? You will not find it easy to say
where the streets are narrower and the freedom
greater for practice and exercise in virtue than in this
Order and in this holy community.* There is greater
freedom for good precisely because there is less
licence for evil. The greater the strictness, the
straighter the way. Narrower streets make wider
squares. So what does it mean—to seek Jesus through
streets and squares—but to restrict and to expand
oneself in this way to capture happiness in his light?

Ps 83:2-3.

*Lam 13, n. 46;
176, n. 141;
195, n. 162.*

7. Do you wish me to apply both squares and streets interiorly to the mind? Do you not agree that he is located in a sort of street, as if in an alley, whose patience is tried, whose chastity is strained and whose charity is straitened? One who does not cultivate any virtue freely and without labor, without toil and anxious striving of spirit, does he not resemble a beggar in the streets? And although such men beg, not without toil, not without effort, yet even they seek repose in him whom their soul loves, as if they sought him through the streets. Of them the prophet says: 'Lord, in straits they sought you', and 'in the path of your judgements, Lord, we awaited you'.*

Is 26:16, 8.

This happens quite often to the untrained and to novices. They are wont to be tried with various temptations or with a kind of tedium,[6] when homesickness constrains them or the attraction of the virtue fails to cheer them. Blessed is one who is not scandalized by these difficulties, who is not cast down, who does not lose Jesus, but rather seeks him through such streets, seeks him in straits, unlike those of whom it is said: 'In straits they sought you; in affliction which made them complain, your teaching came to them'.* Rather such a one recognizes in those straits both occasions for virtue and the teaching of the Father; so he presses on 'courageously from beginning to end',* until he emerges from the streets into the squares.

Is 26:16.

Lm 4:18.

Even those who are more perfect and are accustomed to the squares are sometimes permitted to slip back suddenly into the straits of the streets. Who indeed is more perfect than she who is called his bride? See, she too seeks her Beloved thorugh the streets and some narrow alleys. This difficulty in seeking is not without a purpose, for by it her humility is tested and her desire aroused. How often have I felt myself astray, as it were in a labyrinth of streets, shut up in straits of the spirit, when suddenly I emerged into neighboring squares and the good Lord led me into the open. In the streets I almost gave up the ghost, but in the squares I suddenly

regained my spirit. In these squares some breadth
and freedom of a mind disengaged and unencum-
bered is recommended to you.

8. Take care however not to turn this freedom
into a pretext for the flesh. Take care not to pile
mud in your square, the mud of unlawful thoughts.
Otherwise the Lord will wash you away like mud in
the squares. 'They made our footsteps slip' in the

Ws 8:1.

squares,* says the prophet, meaning that those
squares should be considered muddy in which the
foothold is slippery. Let your squares be paved not
with mud but with gold. Let there be no mud for
you there, nor yet any dryness and aridity, but there
let streams of living water flow, some fountains of
spiritual meditation. In your squares apportion these
waters with the largess of a free mind. Wisdom says:
'Like a plane tree I grew tall by the waters in the

Si 24:19.

squares'.* Not only in the squares nor only by the
waters, but, wisdom says, 'by the waters in the squares
I grew tall'.

So that joyful saplings of wisdom may sprout,
how much assistance do you suppose they need of
carefree leisure and the frequent watering of holy
meditation? Wisdom so planted will grow tall as a
plane tree. O truly blessed are the squares where wisdom grows so tall, rising on high and overtopping all
else, clearly revealed without need for search!

Notice too how some people expose the whole
breadth of their heart to worldly prudence, how they
expand and widen their spirit into a square in order
to plant there a faithless sapling, that is, an alien
seed. How they irrigate it with unflagging exertion

Lam 183, n. 82;
185 nn. 99, 100.

and frequent meditation* and schooling. Hence you
may discover in them the wisdom of this world—
luxuriant, fulsome and towering—and the discretion
of this world, bearing its fruit, but among them the
wisdom which comes from God is lowly and obscure
and impossible to find.

9. Go into the squares and streets of the city.
Examine the leisure, investigate the business of those
who frequent the lawcourts, those who preside and
those who plead before their tribunal. Observe

their actions in public and in the privacy of their
chamber. Does the pure and true wisdom of heaven
tower in their midst? Is the wisdom they treat in
their briefs reflected in their behavior? Will you find
wisdom on display there, towering like a cedar in
Lebanon and like a cypress on Mount Sion? Yes, on
these mountains also wisdom boasts that it grows
tall.* These very names contain a hidden meaning
and the order of the words is not without purpose.
Lebanon comes first in the praise of wisdom and then
Sion is added; after the radiance of a pure heart you
mount to the splendor of the contemplation of
truth. Purity merits acquaintance, not only that derived from books but also an acquaintance sweet and
intimate, infused into the very marrow of the soul. In
Scripture, purity is the ally of truth, its comrade and
its percursor. Therefore wisdom in her praise joins
both mountains, Lebanon and Sion.

    Among those who plead or adjudicate in lawsuits,
will you be able to identify these mountains? Wisdom
cannot be found among men in whom there is no
place for wisdom. But wisdom loves Lebanon, loves
Sion, loves the squares, rejoices in freedom and in the
heights. How great then is the travesty, if that wisdom which frequents the courts and whose motive is
profit towers over everything and hides the wisdom
of God! The wisdom of the courts towers over all,
while that which is modest and peaceful and in harmony with good men is scorned and lurks in a corner.
The former is cultivated, the latter neglected, as if it
were barren and of little profit. A neglected sapling
does not grow tall. Rarely will you find it towering
in the square like a plane tree. It does not strike the
eye and is rarely encountered. So the bride says:
'I sought him but I did not find him'.

    10. Everywhere the name of Jesus is on men's
lips, argued about, venerated. Would that what a
man's voice proclaims, his life would reproduce, his
imitation portray, and his character raise aloft like a
beacon. Let one who seeks wisdom enthroned in
your midst find wisdom at your very gates, in your
very senses, in the moderation and composure of

Si 24:17.

your outward bearing. For your senses are like gates
through which comes an inkling of the one who
dwells within. From your fruits is known whether
Jesus dwells with you. The bride approaches you, she
turns over the leaves of your fig tree, looks for fruit
in you, looks for her Beloved. For this is the fruit
sweet to her palate. Happy are you when you have
plenty of this fruit, when you give the bride of your
Lord her fill of this nourishment. Her food is a chosen
food. Her delight is that her Beloved should be with
you. She is not envious; she is not jealous. She
wishes her Beloved to be the Beloved of all. She seeks
him in all, either to find him in all or to invite him to
all. For she seeks Jesus with those whose progress she
seeks in him. She seeks him through the streets and
squares but she cannot find him in all of them.

'I sought him', she says, 'but I have not found
him'. Paul thirsted for the salvation of all; he longed
to find Christ in the hearts of all, as he yearned for all

Ph 1:8.

in the heart of Christ.* But listen to what he says;
hear how he complains of some: 'I have no one with
the same spirit' as Timothy, . . . 'all seek their own

Ph 2:20-21; see
Lam 7, n. 14.

interests, not those of Jesus Christ'.*

Do you think that Christ can be found with those
who do not seek to find him? In fact, you will find
many who in this way seek something other than himself, yet through him. He is made the subject of a
treatise in councils, of a debate in courts, of a disputation in the schools, of a song in churches. These
preoccupations are religious. But go to the harbor
mouth and consider the result of this stream of
activity. See if all this is not a kind of haggling over
the price of Christ. It is a lucrative business, the
name of Christ. Nothing is more prized, nothing
more desirable. Happy nonetheless is he who prizes
the excellence of this name.

Among others let there be treatises, lawsuits, dis-
putations about this name. For us it is enough if, in

Lam 14, n. 53.

our cloisters at least, this name be loved.* Nowhere
else is the opportunity greater and therefore nowhere
else is the embarrassment greater, if Christ be not
found under our roof.[7] The fair form of justice is

not found if the intention of pious works is not
pure. For joyousness itself is a kind of divine eagerness of mind, which is usually conceived in his
presence and which we can really interpret as his
presence. This heavenly and transcendent affection,
I say, is no easy matter to be met with at every step.
This particularly the bride means I think, when she
says: 'I sought but have not found him whom my
soul loves', Christ Jesus, who lives and reigns for ever
and ever. Amen.

NOTES TO SERMON FIVE

1. Reading *tam dulcia* for *jam dulcia* with Migne.
2. For this classical passage on scriptural meditation see Lam 182 n. 76.
3. Reading *accensum* with Mab. for *ascensum* with Migne.
4. *Ergo vacationis et laetitiae usus in plateis est.* See Lam 21, n. 93.
5. Reading *primo* with Migne for *prima* with Mab.
6. See Lam 196-98. G. explores the opposite of affectionate love or consolation under various but overlapping names: *tedium* or boredom generally accompanied by sadness, *tristitia. Tedium* and *tristitia* are used more frequently than *acedia,* which Cassian defines as *tedium* or fretfulness of heart (PL 49: 359-60). To these G. adds *fastidium,* disdain, distaste, disgust; *acerbitas* bitterness of fruit; and *amaritudo,* bitterness of heart. G. thinks of these in various metaphors for stormy weather; tempest, whirlwind, especially the north wind. G. returns frequently to this topic to give understanding, consolation and remedy: S 5:7, 6:1, 14:3, 16:8, 17:2, 6; 21:2; 26:5; 38:5-6; 39:5; 40:1, 7, 9: 45: 6; T 1:1; T 2:4.
7. Lam 20, nn. 88, 89; 195, n. 168; Jean Leclercq in SAn 31 (1953) 20, n. 3, and his *Vocabulaire Monastique,* SAn 48 (1961) 164.

SERMON 6,
THE WATCHMEN'S VISIONS

*Fervent love is detected by good watchmen.
1. Fervent and persevering prayer is necessary.
2-3. Lovers need spiritual watchmen for spiritual discernment; 4-5. various watchmen have seen the Lord before the Incarnation, after the Incarnation, by faith and by grace. 6. How watchmen should report to the bride.*

HAVE YOU SEEN HIM WHOM MY SOUL LOVES?[1]   *Sg 3:3*

The bride suffers delay in her search and the Bridegroom casts over her a shadow of perplexity, for he does not at once grant access to his presence. Nonetheless she continues her eagerness with fervent zeal and redoubles her lament: 'I have not found him'. Brothers, if eagerness is repulsed, when will idleness be welcome? If love does not find, when will lukewarmness, neglect of prayer or slackness find him? Now why do I discuss neglect of prayer and slackness among you? There is no need to apply a remedy for a malady you have not contracted. These vices are foreign to you. For who among you is not frequently and fervently at prayer? If there is no listlessness, however, take care lest the tedium of delay weary and exhaust your desires. A charge may be laid against you in either case: if your soul is slack in petition or lax in hope. You hear that the desires of the bride were delayed, and at the first rebuff in prayer, do you petulantly complain that you are not inundated with the delights of divine

97

Mt 26:40.

Mt 24:42. See
Lam p. 181, n. 67;
190 nn. 133, 134;
192, n. 145.

inspiration? You have only now begun and is your
spirit so quickly deflected from its course? What
if that reproach in the Gospel were brought against
you: 'So you could not watch with me one hour'?*
'Watch then and pray, for you do not know at what
hour' your Beloved may come.*

Dogged prayer reaches its goal. And if at the
beginning prayer seems to you dry and stony, still
from this hardest of rocks you will squeeze the oil of
grace if only you persevere, if protracted delay does
not sap your strength, if your longings do not grow
slack from deferral. Deferral is obviously painful to a
lover but desires prolonged grow stronger. Why do I
harp on what you know? Recurring frustration will
give you, indeed many a time has given you, an understanding of prayer. I have frequently found you well
versed in the pursuit of prayer. I cannot boast that I
have engendered these affections in you, yet I rejoice
to have found you in them. And if I have not formed
these interests in you, may I at least encourage you in
them! I am a watchman. That is why you often repeat
to me the question of the bride: 'Have you seen him
whom my soul loves'? O blessed soul, exercised by
desires so holy! These are the desires of the beloved, a
beloved able to enquire only about Christ, for when
discovered by the watchmen, she blurts out this inquiry: 'Have you seen him whom my soul loves'?

2. The bride of the Canticle is met preoccupied
with her inquiries: 'The city watchmen' she says,
Sq 3:3.
'have found me'.* Imposters and mountebanks dread
nothing so much as detection by watchmen and
if they are caught they are not easily convicted. Cain
became a vagabond and an outcast on earth because
he dreaded detection: 'Whoever finds me' he said,
Gn 4:14.
'will slay me'.* He does not wish his sin to be slain,
he does not wish to suffer wholesome confusion
in confession, the healing chastisement of a master.
He does not wish to be detected because he does not
wish to die. Now where undisciplined affection does
not fear to be slain but rather is assured of protec-
tion, it vaunts itself wantonly. But the bride presents
herself voluntarily. She goes gladly to meet the

Bridegroom's comrades. Why not be glad? She is detected not as one fleeing an avenger but as one seeking a lover.

'The watchmen found me'. They have not been found but have found. Herein their diligence is commended. Indolent and unreliable watchmen fail in diligence on this point; they do not make the rounds, they do not seek to detect anyone whose conscience has been cauterized with a burning ember and who betrays the fires of affection by the sign of chaste love and by eagerness in seeking the Beloved. They do not meet with their subjects and perhaps are annoyed if their subjects interrupt them. Some utter a word of consolation only if questioned and others not even then. Such a watchman only repeats the literal meaning of a text; he adds nothing from his experience or his care of souls. The task of a watchman is obviously something more: he must not only reform but also provide; not only await but rather inspire inquirers; as if from a lookout he must look over his sons for any one who has understanding and is seeking God.* I am your watchman; give me a trained tongue, O Lord, that I may know how to sustain by the word and direct towards the word one who has fallen.

Ps 13:2; RB 7:27.

3. And what else does the bride want when she says: 'Have you seen him whom my soul loves'? You see her not so much wearied as stimulated by spiritual pursuits.* You have understood her doggedness in pursuing her Beloved; now observes her humble She knows not how to disregard the watchmen. Nor does she think it safe to pass by without consulting those whom she knows not only share the Lord's counsel but also bear his command. 'Have you seen him whom my soul loves'? Yet what is the meaning of a question phrased so ambiguously? Did she wish thereby to warn you not to trust every spirit but to discern whether the spirit is from God?*

Lam p. 177, n. 43.

1 Jo 4:1.

Not all of those who have either shouldered or seized the job of watchman can give reliable witness of the Bridegroom. For there are many whose 'eye is upon the whole earth' and, according to a verse in Proverbs, 'upon the ends of the earth'.* The light

Zc 5:6; Pr 17:24.

of the eye is not with them; they are unable to thrust it beyond the bounds of earth or to lift it to heaven. They are indeed reliable and busy enough, but only in amassing and hoarding earthly goods. 'Their eye' says the prophet, 'is upon the whole earth'. Insatiable greed extends over the whole earth. Accordingly, a mind made gross by earthly cares and by providing a table of that food which perishes,[2] does not know how to dispense some viaticum from his heavenly banquet for his subjects' benefit and to reflect some clear truth from his heavenly contemplation. In fact if such watchmen are perhaps asked about mysteries of the spirit, they answer that the plain way of faith and morals is sufficient. In this way they console themselves for their own sterility or they measure the avidity of others by their own tepidity. For a love listless and lax, with blameworthy patience, does not so much yearn for as wait for future blessings, whereas a watchman of greater fervor is swept on by burning desire and attempts to filch a flower or two from the bouquet reserved for him.

Because the bride knows such watchmen are very numerous, she weighs her question in a delicate balance: 'Have you seen him whom my soul loves?' A watchman may be prudent, faithful, painstaking, and by careful concern for discipline may ward off from his fold the intrusion of enemies. Yet he will not forthwith know how to sing love songs nor as the Bridegroom's courtier announce his 'presence nor, suddenly swept into his private chamber, emerge with some precious drops of interior delight. For these are two quite different graces, on the one hand to detect the shifty and counterfeit pandering of an adulterer and on the other to arrange the lawful visits of the Bridegroom. Since experience of evil is frequent, knowledge of evil is easy. But because experience of spiritual encounters is rare and because judgement about them is delicate, evidence about them is quite tenuous and spiritual meanings can be discerned only by spiritual men. Therefore they can be explained only by spiritual men, such as those of whom Isaiah says: 'How beautiful on the mountains are the feet of those who proclaim peace, proclaim good news'.* *Is 52:7. See Miquel p. 157, n. 23.*

4. 'Have you seen him whom my soul loves?' The sight of the Bridegroom is not one, or simple, or uniform. Abraham danced to see his day: 'he saw it and rejoiced'.[3] Jacob saw the Lord face to face and his life was spared.* Moses saw him, but only his back.* Isaiah saw the Lord seated on a lofty throne.† Ezechiel saw him.* Daniel saw him in the likeness of man† although He had not yet assumed human nature. But every vision of this kind before the Incarnation was revealed in bodily appearance but not in the reality of a human body. The apostles saw him in the very reality of the flesh and they touched and handled him. *Gn 32:31.*

*Ex 33:23.
†Is 6:1.
*Ezk 1.
†Dn 7:13.*

Yet both the former and the latter saw God inwardly by faith. He said to Philip: 'he who sees me, sees also my Father'.* That this sight is a matter of faith is made clear by what follows: 'Do you not believe that I am in the Father and the Father is in me? . . . If not my words, accept the evidence of my deeds'.* To prove that Philip sees the Father, the Lord argues that Philip sees the Son; what conclusion follows except that the Lord meant Philip's vision of both Father and Son to be understood as the vision of God through faith. So the Lord adds to the argument for belief: 'Do you not believe that I am in the Father and the Father is in me? . . . If not my words, accept the evidence of my deeds.' For if Christ dwells 'in our hearts by faith',* and if those hearts of ours are cleansed by faith, why is He not also seen in our hearts by faith? As for the visions mentioned previously, some given in a likeness, others in the flesh, both sets are full of delight or of profit, but completeness is reserved for the third set of visions, those given through faith.[4] *Jn 14:9.*

Jn 14:10-11.

Ep 3:17; Ac 15:9.

5. For to speak of the appearance of the Word which took place in the flesh, besides the words of life which issued from his mouth, what singular marks of excellence do you think shone from his visible features! What obvious indications of the

excellence within were given by his eye, his voice, his
face! In scripture, how every gesture communicated a
divine grace! Joyful indeed was that vision, but for
one who believed that God was present in the man.
And indeed that vision accorded the prophets and
patriarchs before the Incarnation of Christ did com-
municate something divine in his visible likeness, as I
believe, and it poured incalculable joy into the mind
and senses of the beholder. The vision was brought
before the eyes only of those whose spirit was pure.
Even after his resurrection, he is said to have appeared in the reality of his flesh only to the
Ac 10:40-41.   'witnesses God had chosen beforehand'.*

Happy are those watchmen, if there are any to
whom such a vision appears frequently and fami-
liarly, especially a vision which shows him in his
glorified body, as Peter and John saw him trans-
Mt 17:1-2.   figured on the mountain.* Yet that earlier vision was
not the reality and this latter not the full reality. For
by that earlier vision Moses was joyfully engaged but
Ex 33:13, 18-21.   not fully satisfied. 'Show me yourself', said Moses.*
But about the Transfiguration the Lord himself said:
'It is for your good that I am going'. Otherwise, 'the
Jn 16:7.   Advocate will not come'.* Good is that vision then
which our Advocate brings at his coming; it is spiri-
tual because given inwardly by the Spirit. Then
against Christ the Lord is spirit before our face.[5]

This vision exists either in truth revealed spiritually through the understanding or in sweetness
infused by grace. For this latter experience is also to
see. 'Taste and see', says the psalmist, 'that the Lord
Ps 33:9.   is sweet'.* Most sweet certainly is this vision and
although not yet full compared with the vision to
come, [it is] yet near that fullness; it is near in
quality if not in equality. This vision is not subject
to human talent nor proposed for the grasp of human
effort, although it is sometimes freely bestowed on
human longing. In short, since this vision is not conceived by the power of the intellect, it cannot
prolong its stay uninterruptedly in the mind's memory. It is instantaneous. It is its own master. It comes
and goes with the rush of a mighty wind. It is sudden

and instantaneous, abruptly arriving and abruptly departing. And if it is momentary, there linger on embers of thought as burning as they are bright and they keep holiday in the spirit of the one who remembers. The memory remains of the vision tasted and savored; those who can savor its sweetness know how to recall it, especially at the hour of prayer. For a heart still aglow with recent grace recollects one good word and in fervent meditation pours forth similar expressions.* For this heart savors much of the inner sweetness in individual words, and its expressions are most attractive for they well up from grace abounding.

Lam p. 185, n. 102 and Miquel p. 156, n. 20.

6. If you are a watchman, realize that you must have such expressions ready for the arrival of the bride. Why meet her, if you do not come to announce some delicious or fresh news? If you have nothing new, offer what is old. Present what she knows, if you have no news. But nothing is presented if it must be extorted. She does not ask in what guise you saw him but whether you saw him. It suffices to present him in the guise she knows. Yet it brings an increase of grace if you announce something new. Then again what is neither unknown nor unfamiliar to her meditation becomes sweet to the bride by a new grace. The ear does not tire when the heart is on fire; only talk about the Bridegroom and you have offered something novel for the ears of his bride.

You do not always have an answer ready from that surpassing and transcendent mode of vision. It is sublime and subtle and wont suddenly to take possession of the spirit which it finds pure and free from distraction. It takes possession suddenly but it does not remain in possession for long. These subtle matters are not at one's beck and call; but a watchman can share some simple delicacy.[6] Each and every article of faith presented with some tasty seasoning of explanation begets in the hearer the sweetest of affections and transports of the mind. The bride is fastidious; she prefers what is delicious to what is overpowering, except that she 'is capable of all

Ph 4:13.

Ps 36:30.

Ml 2:7.

things in him who strengthens her',* the Bridegroom. Let others tell stories or dwell on controversies. Let your 'lips dwell on wisdom and your tongue speak' delights, you who speak to the bride.* For she also wants watchmen ready to relate the biography and the good news of her Beloved. The lips of priests should safeguard knowledge; therefore she demands the law from their mouth,* the law of seeing and finding her Beloved.

'Have you seen him whom my soul loves?' As a result of their seeing him, she assumes that she will see him; therefore she diligently inquires into the watchmen's vision, hoping by talking with them either to be led to his hiding place or to be touched by greater sweetness. For this is to see him whom she loves, to conceive with eager affection and pure mind the Wisdom and the Power of God. Well does that man behold him who conceives him in both ways, with pure gaze and devout affection. Soft, I think, are the whispers exchanged between the bride and the watchmen and pleasant their conference, if it can be called a conference, for no answer on their part is mentioned here. If any there be, it is very secret, a secret which she judges must be wrapped in deep silence. It is her own secret, all her own. Neither do we hazard a guess here about an answer the bride took pains to suppress. With their silence let us now conclude our sermon, postponing for tomorrow the passage of the bride in which she says that she passed on a little beyond the watchmen and found him whom her soul loves.

NOTES TO SERMON SIX

1.   The sermon is addressed to one person throughout, with adaptations in the plural in paragraph 1, which praise the community of Swineshead.

2.   Jo 6:27, reading *cibi* for *sibi* with the Florentine ed.

3.   Jn 8:56. Aelred (Oner III; PL 195:368-9) divides *visio* into six kinds: *sensualis, imaginaria, phantastica, spiritualis, rationalis, intellectualis.* Aelred and G. are equally scriptural but neither shows dependence on the other in discussing the same word, *visio.*

4.   Jn 14:9-12. See A. Van den Bosch, 'Christ and the Christian Faith according to St. Bernard', Citeaux 12 (1961) 105-119, 193-210.

5.   Lm 4:20; G. *spiritus ante faciem nostram Christus Dominus;* Vulg. *Spiritus oris nostri, christu dominus,* Jer. Bible 'The breath of our nostrils, Yahweh's anointed'. See J. Danielou, 'Saint Bernard et les Peres grecs', SBT 48-51.

6.   *dulcia non deducit in medium,* Mab.; Migne and the Florentine ed. omit *non,* as in this translation.

SERMON 7,
APPROACH THE BELOVED

*Love passes beyond the watchmen to the
Beloved. 1. Seek the Bridegroom with heart
purified, prompt and importunate. 2. To read
about him is no substitute for colloquy. 3. Love
passes by the witness and example of others to
reach towards him. 4. As man, he surpasses all
generations in righteousness and integrity.
5. Not the Synagogue but the Church passes
on by faith to his divinity, and finds him the
good Samaritan. 6. The soul of Christ surpasses
angelic spirits. 7. Glorious is the raiment of his
flesh; 8. and gloriously new is his raiment in
the sacrament of the altar. 9. His visible works
are surpassed by the gifts of his soul.*

WHEN I HAD PASSED BY A LITTLE BEYOND
THEM, I FOUND HIM WHOM MY SOUL LOVES[1]   *Sg 3:4.*

You are importunate creditors and demand
payment from your debtor too relentlessly. Yet that is pardonable, provided
you ask for your due. But you demand
that I pay a debt I have not incurred. I was about to
treat of the passing on of the bride. For to this I am
bound by orderly sequence and by my promise,
whereas with the bride you still insist on asking me:
'Have you seen him whom my soul loves?'*   *Sg 3:3.*
She moderates her enquiry with greater restraint as if

hesitant, asking rather than insisting. For she knows that it is not granted to everyone to speak about this vision, nor at all times. For once He hides his face, who may contemplate him?

Yet you urge me to lay down for you some rule for contemplating the Beloved and to give you a method for this discovery and vision. What does this mean? Would you have me confine within a rule the bounty of God's gift? This vision results not from human effort but from grace. It is the fruit of revelation, not of research. If, however, effort can contribute to this end, observe first the advice of Isaiah: *Is 1:16.* 'Wash, make yourselves clean'.* Secondly, write about wisdom in your time of leisure, for he who is *Sir 38:25.* relieved of other tasks will acquire wisdom.* Thirdly, be violent and capture the joy of the kingdom too *Mt 11:12; see* long withheld from you.* So you are advised to keep *Miquel p. 155,* your heart purified, prompt and importunate. By the *n. 17.* first you will become worthy, by the second devout, by the third eager; that is worthy, attentive and insistent: worthy to welcome grace, meeting it on the way, impatient when it delays. By the first you are prepared; by the second you are likened to the bride as she waits for her Beloved to return from the wedding feast; by the third you hasten, just as the bride who does not wait but hastens and bypasses even the watchmen.

I would have done better to say 'passes by'. For what we bypass, we do not observe or approach but rather disregard, whereas what we pass by, we intend to examine, to question and to probe. Nor is this passing by profitless. For when the bride had passed on a little, she found her Beloved. Do you see, brothers, how much it profits [us] to consult the watchmen? It guides the devout but errant soul to discover her Beloved. Consultation is profitable indeed, and often what the erudition of the counsellor does not provide is merited by the humility of the petitioner. It is good for you to be earnest but not relentless in such inquiry. For even the bride questions the watchmen, not so much by design but as chance offers and in passing. Love for her Beloved drew her onward and did not allow her a pause to confer at leisure with the watchmen. She continued to run, her heart athirst, catching her breath perhaps, thanks to the proximity of the Bridegroom. So she paid less heed to those who blessed her in word and sped on to him who blesses in spirit, who is God blessed above all forever.

2. Pay heed to this, you who pray on the run but dally with books, you who are fervent in reading and lukewarm in praying. Reading should serve prayer, should dispose the affections, should neither devour the hours nor gobble up the moments of prayer. When you read you are taught about Christ, but when you pray you join him in familiar colloquy.[2]. How much more enchanting is the grace of speaking with him than about him! But if those who indulge too passionately in reading suffer some loss in spiritual visitations from infrequent prayer, what shall we say of those who are either dissipated by uncontrolled conversation or distracted by worrisome disputation? According to the Rule, a monk's role is not to chat but to observe silence; his quest is not for questions but for quiet.[3] Or if any disquiet is to be welcome, it should be that of love not of contention.

Holy love indeed has its own disquiet, but such as you read about in Isaiah: 'I will not be silent . . . nor be quiet until the just one comes forth like the dawn and the saviour flares out like a torch'.* Does not the bride suggest a similar anxiety of spirit when she says; 'When I had passed beyond them'? She was swept on by the impulse of fervent love and therefore admits that she passed on, as if surpassing in avidity and desire anything words could convey. 'When I had passed them by, I found him whom my soul loves.' She passed them by either by sifting their teaching or by evaluating their nature. She passed by both what could be said by them and what could be seen in them. For whoever these watchmen may be, although they be in your interpretation either Cherubim or Seraphim, they can neither expose in speech nor express by imitation all that concerns Christ. 'All things are difficult and man is unable to explain them

Is 62:1.

Qo 1:8.

in speech.'* If there is such difficulty with creatures, who shall speak worthily or fully of their Creator? So the bride says: 'When I had passed them by'.

3. Would that we might be such hearers of the word of God as not to be overwhelmed by the message through either slowness of wit or lukewarmness of desire, lest the message outstrip both our appetite and our capacity. But let us pass by this effort rather of a teacher than of an admonitor, and although we may not yet grasp, let us divine or at least desire greater gifts. For in one sense the man who pursues larger game, though he may not capture it at once, passes beyond what is presented to him.[4] But the bride did capture hers; therefore she sings out joyfully:[5] 'When I had passed them by, I found him whom my soul loves'.

Why should she not pass by those whose knowledge is limited and whose nature is finite? Indeed he who is sought is great and immense and no other is comparable to him. He cannot then be fairly evaluated by the witness or example of anyone else. Everyone else can be passed by; he alone can not be passed by. He says: 'Come to me all you who desire me, and be filled with my fruits'.* 'Come to me', he says, not 'Pass me by'. For in what way can that be passed by which is boundless? Full measure, says Luke, shaken together, pressed down, overflowing, will be poured into your lap.* To you Immensity is dispensed in measure, but in itself Immensity is immeasurable. Luke does not say 'full' but 'overflowing'. If then the measure cannot be contained, when will Immensity itself be contained? How will it be possible to pass by that which cannot be fully contained? In the Canticle, the bride has no desire to pass by but says: 'I held him fast, nor would I let him go'.* 'When I had passed by a little beyond them, I found him whom my soul loves.' Perhaps these watchmen whom she passed a little beyond before finding her Beloved were closely related to the Bridegroom. But if we mean 'closely related' according to his divine nature, who among created spirits approaches anywhere near that Immensity and Ma-

Si 24:26.

Lk 6:38.

Sg 3:4.

jesty? For even if some likeness is ascribed to them, it is recognized as far inferior and very unlike. For no one exists like you, O Lord. Perhaps then this proximity, which nature excludes, knowledge makes possible.

4. But who would be rash enough to proclaim that the unfathomable abyss of divine wisdom can be plumbed by the intellect of a created spirit? 'He dwells', says Paul, 'in light inaccessible'.* Though he is inaccessible to us, we are not inaccessible to his light. So Isaiah says: 'I have brought my justice near' and my salvation will not be delayed.* Justice has been brought near because made incarnate; nearer because revealed; but yet brought nearest because freely conferred. The justice of God the Father, Christ Jesus was brought near by his assumption of our flesh. But he outstripped every generation of mankind by a twofold prerogative in his relationship to the state of human nature, by his righteousness and by his integrity. For apart from him no one is clear of defilement, no one immune from corruption. He was endowed then with this twofold gift and he outstripped his fellows.

Accordingly, let your faith also pass by all others, that in him alone you may weigh the level of justice and the integrity of the nature you share with him. Yet do pass on a little, for as he far outstrips us in justice and freedom from corruption, so he has been brought near by sharing a nature not different from ours. In their estimate of him the Jews did not know how to pass beyond Moses, Abraham and the other patriarchs or prophets, because they considered him to be like one of the others and not to possess any surpassing grace. In John, they insisted: 'Abraham and the prophets are dead and do you say:"He who eats my flesh will not die for ever? Who do you claim to be?" '* They refused to go beyond the Baptist but concluded: John is the Christ.* Yet John did not allow them to stop at himself but disclaimed the opinion of him they adopted through lack of faith: 'I am not the Christ', said John, 'but in your midst stands one whom you do not know'.*

1 Tm 6:16.

Is 46:13.

Jn 8:52-53.
Lk 3:15.

Jn 1:20.

Ps 44:8.

' 5. The Synagogue knows not how to pass on, but evaluated him by the standard of the others and charged him with blasphemy because, man as he was, he made himself out to be God. But the faith of the Church did pass on and discovered him anointed with the 'oil of gladness more than his fellows'.* And with what oil abounding was he anointed! From his bounty he poured oil into all our wounds! Yes, we are the wounded man who went down to Jericho, fell among brigands, was robbed, and wounded and left half dead. Too many passed by and there was not one to save his life. That great patriarch Abraham passed by, for he was not the one to justify but only justified through faith in the one to come. Moses passed by, for he was not the giver of grace but the lawgiver, giver of that Law which leads no one to the perfect one.* For justice does not come from the Law.† Aaron passed by. The priest passed by, and by the same victims which he offered unceasingly he was unable to 'cleanse men's consciences from dead works to serve the living God'.* Patriarch, pontiff and prophet passed by, as barren in spirit as in deed; indeed in the wounded man, they also were wounded.

Heb 7:19; see
Lam p. 195,
n. 167.
†Rm 3:20; Ga
2:21; 3:21.

Heb 9:14.
RB 46:5-6.

At the sight of the wounded only that true Samaritan is moved with compassion, is all compassion; he poured oil into wounds, himself into hearts, cleansing by faith the hearts of all. So the faith of the Church passed beyond all men and comes to him who alone could not pass her by, but set her on his beast* and was himself made a beast of burden. Yes, she passes on a little to discover him whom she believes to be so free from corruption that she proclaims him one who shares her state. She so considers him the author of grace that she confesses him to be a partaker in her nature.

Lk 10:30-34.

6. Now if we should say he far outstrips even those angelic spirits of heaven by virtue of the most holy soul which was his possession, this will not be repugnant to faith but entirely consonant with the dignity of his person. For if he was made a little less than the angels* on account of the flesh with which he was clothed, yet he is their equal in his

Heb 2:9.

spiritual substance and their superior in his prerogative of excellence. Therefore O bride, pass by the
angels also. They too are your watchmen and
guardians, for they say through Jeremiah, 'We tried
to cure Babylon but she has not been healed'.* Pass *Jr 51:9.*
by them, I say, and in your Beloved contemplate the
endowments of his unique privilege. They are min-
istering spirits, not the cause of salvation,[6] whereas
he is the Angel of great counsel 'who accomplished
our salvation in the midst of the earth'.* Therefore *Jr 32:19;*
God exalted him and gave him a name above *Ps 73:12.*
every name.* *Ph 2:9.*

Joyous contemplation it is in the family of heaven
to gaze upon simplicity of essence, serenity of mind
and the sweetness of mutual love. Joyous contemplation it is to gaze upon everlasting existence, purity
of understanding, depth of knowledge, and also upon
humility in obedience, tranquillity in diligence, ease
in achievement.* Yet pass by them all and behold the *Lam p. 16, n. 59.*
great stature of the one who enters to save the
nations. Hymns of angels escort him as he enters
earth's orbit and on his triumphal return angels welcome him with a canticle of wonder: 'Who is this
coming from Edom, from Bozrah in crimsoned gar-
ments, one glorious in his apparel?'* the apparel of *Is 63:1.*
his own flesh!

7. Rightly glorious is he in this apparel, which
was conceived without intercourse, born of the
Virgin, kept immune not only from corruption but
even from the seeds of corruption, not rent in the
tomb, raised again on the third day, taken up into
heaven on the fortieth day, and every day (a wonder
to be loved above all else) offered to believers as food
for their salvation!* Who would not wonder lovingly *Lam p. 172, n. 16.*
at each of these marvels and ask: 'Who is this so
glorious in his apparel?' You have hastened through
all these kinds of marvels[7] or rather you have stood
still in amazement at each of them severally, and
suddenly a fresh source of wonder arises for you.
You would have been sufficiently moved by the
marvels related already; here again you are roused to
amazement, as if that verse of Isaiah were said to

Is 43:18-19;
Rev 21:5.

you: 'Remember not the former things; I am making things new'.*

8. What could be newer than this marvel that in the mystery of the Lord's Body the matter is changed while the appearance is preserved? The original appearance remains but there exists a new grace because there exists a new substance. New indeed not in itself but in its outward appearance, clearly new because the substance of the Lord's flesh, received in an appearance not its own, bestows on the soul the power of sanctification and in that his immaculate flesh in the mystery of the altar purifies our spiritual substance. This is indeed new and beyond what occurs in other sacraments, because not only a new grace of sanctification is granted but also because the natural substance is changed. For by the blessing of the sacrament, the bread which is offered undergoes this ineffable change and by sacramental consecration and by union with the living Word, this life-giving grace flows back into Christ's flesh.[8] For 'the flesh is of no avail; it is the spirit which gives life',* bestowing on the sacred flesh in the august sacrament spiritual efficacy for imparting life to those who partake of so great a mystery.

Jn 6:64.

'Glorious therefore is he in his apparel', that is, in his flesh, but much more glorious in the spirit he assumed, which to be sure is more excellent than the flesh because nearer to the Word. Understand that in his spirit 'he is anointed more than his fellows': that is, not only more than the children of men but also more than the angelic hosts. Why should not he, more than they, be anointed with the oil of grace, who, not like others by participation but by personal union, is entwined with that most fruitful olive tree from which all unction flows? Does the Truth and the Word of God not seem to you like an olive tree, when his anointing teaches us about all things, when his words are more healing than oil, when his name is oil poured out?* Entwined with this divine olive tree by union in one person, he became, if I may say so, the wild olive which shares our nature and its fruitfulness but not its corruption.

Sg 1:2.

9. What light, what savor, what sweetness, what excellence of every kind he received the evidence of his works gives witness, except that what he experienced in his spirit far excelled what he expressed by his deeds. In the light of all the external evidence of his excellence, you may exclaim with the bride: 'your name is as oil poured out', 'not to mention what lies hidden within'.* For it is not fitting that any external action, however marvellous, should match the excellence of his soul. I cannot comprehend, Lord, all your works though they are exposed to view. They are of surpassing excellence and it is beyond me to evaluate them. How then should I experience the grace which lies hidden within? Eye has not seen, O most blessed soul of Christ, without your help, the gifts divinely bestowed upon you. Therefore the angelic spirits, failing to comprehend, do not cease to marvel and, as if ignorant but in amazement, break into the hymn of praise already quoted: 'Who is this so glorious in his apparel, striding in the greatness of his might?'

Sg 1:2, 4:1, 3.

Considering this prerogative of the virtues in her Beloved, the bride rightly admits that she passed by the watchmen and passed by a little way; for she so marvels at the unique grace in him that she nonetheless recognizes that his nature is shared with her and that the blessed soul of Christ is of the same kind as others but of superior and surpassing excellence. I was preparing to expound to you still another passage, but as the subject matter opportunely suggests or rather demands, the sermon shies away from it and hastens to its end. Let us meanwhile remain at the place we have reached, in order that from this level when leisure is available, we may pass on to higher mysteries of the Church's Bridegroom, Jesus Christ, who lives and reigns for ever and ever. Amen.

NOTES TO SERMON SEVEN

1.   The second plural is used in par. 1, first sentence of par. 2 and last two sentences of par. 9; second person singular recurs frequently: *sis* (par. 1), *legis* . . . *seris* . . . *seris* . . . *interpreteris* (par. 2), *perpendas* . . . *pertransi* (par. 4), *cucurristi* . . . *stupidus* . . . *substitisti* . . . *fueris* . . . *excitaris* (par. 7), *intellige* (par. 8).

2.   Lam p. 187, nn. 114, 115; Georges Marie, 'Familiarite avec Dieu', DSp 5 (1964) 50-51.

3.   Leclercq, *Otia Monastica*, 103:3; Lam p. 175, n. 33; 176, n. 41; 180 nn. 60, 61; 181, n. 67.

4.   Reading *qui* for *quid*.

5.   Reading *laeta* for *electa*.

6.   Reading *operarii* for *operari*, with Mab.

7.   Reading *admirationis* with Mab. for *administrationis* with Migne.

8.   *haec vivificatrix gratia in carnem Christi redundat.*

SERMON 8,
CHARITY ASCENDS TO UNDERSTANDING

Love bridges the gap between the human and divine. 1. The bride finds in her Bridegroom both natures integrally, the divine, and the human with body, soul and spirit. 2. He assumes a rational soul, that we might be fully reformed in him. 3. Is the knowledge of the soul of Christ and the knowledge of the Word one and the same? 4-5. Is the wisdom of all the same? 6. How is the divinity close to us? 7. What is the meaning of the image of God in a rational creature? 8. The bride's circuit is complete; a summary of the first eight sermons.

WHEN I HAD PASSED ON A LITTLE BEYOND THEM I FOUND HIM WHOM MY SOUL LOVES*[1]   *Sg 3:4.*

Y ou have passed on, O bride of the Lord, beyond your watchmen, his companions and associates; companions by nature, associates by grace. You have passed them by and come to your Beloved. Why should you not pass by those who themselves would also pass by like smoke, if they did not abide in their Beloved? You have found your Beloved and found him 'anointed with the oil of the Spirit more than his fellows'.*   You have contemplated in him certain   *Ps 44:8.* privileges of excellence in a nature like your own. You have found that his holy soul possesses some gifts uniquely, other gifts pre-eminently. You passed by the watchmen because you preferred him; you admit that you passed on only a little, because the reason for your preference is still founded on fellowship in the same race. But will you stop here? A departure must be made from this level to further and higher things; one must reach the end. Wisdom indeed 'reaches from end to end'.*

Ws 8:1.

The heretic too, without according a higher level to your Beloved, deprives him of this level.[2] He unites only the flesh with the Word in Christ, and denies him a soul; or if he does not dare to deny this (because of the manifest testimony of Christ himself who says: 'No one takes my soul from me but I lay it down'* and take it up again) he grants him a soul responsible for sensation but denies him a rational spirit. He has corrected his error in part but could not withdraw further from the darkness of Egypt. He could not complete the 'three days' journey'.* The faith of the Church has defined in Christ a humanity that is neither alone nor halved. That faith places both natures together in Christ. Because the divine nature is simple and free from all distinction, in his human nature faith confesses that threefold distinction of Paul, that is, body, soul and spirit in their entirety.* Otherwise he did not take upon himself the human nature which he intended to reform in himself. Scripturally, the rational part of the human soul also stood in need of the Mediator's healing, because the soul was darkened by the cloud of ignorance and aglow with the spark of concupiscence. Christ's Church professes that both natures, the human and the divine, are in Christ integrally and, like the woman in the Gospel, the Church stores the leaven of divine wisdom in three measures of human flour.*

Jn 10:18.

Gn 30:36.

1 Th 5:23.

Lk 13:21.

2. But why? Did Christ, himself the Word of the Father and Wisdom and Truth, stand in need of a rational spirit? There could be nothing which escaped his attention but he personally 'enlightens every man coming into this world'.* For what reason then did the light which creates and enlightens need a spirit created and enlightened? For no reason at all. He has no need, but this need is mine. The reason derives

Jn 1:9.

from my blindness, not from his brilliance;[3] the reason lies not in the Word who assumes a human spirit but in the spirit which is assumed. I stood in need, that this part also of my nature should be united with the Word and that thus the merits of the part illumined in God should flood back on all men through faith.

We are all reformed in Christ, the Mediator who shares our nature, whenever we approach him through faith. Therefore the whole man had to be assumed, in order that grace might flood back into the whole, for corruption had fermented the whole. In the one person then there remain two natures, in their integrity and without confusion. For the divine nature is unchangeable and immutable; it can neither be changed into another nor allow another to be changed into it. Neither can it decline from its own into a nature other than its own. For every change in it would be a decline, nor is there any greater possibility that another nature be elevated to the divine nature. We cannot change it but only share in it, by participation certainly but not by essence.[4]

3. Both his natures then retain at once their integrity and their distinguishing characteristics. Consequently the understandings and affections and contemplations and beatitudes which are proper to each are also unmingled, distinct and different and can be numbered without multiplication of his person. For who would assert that the most blessed soul of Christ has no deep feeling of sweetness and joy? Or again who would allow his soul that inmost taste of sweetness and savor and beatitude which the most Blessed Trinity enjoys?[5] For it is of greater excellence to be than to share that living goodness,[6] and there is a much fuller and more intimate experience in Being Itself than in the enjoyment of being. To Exist is indeed to enjoy Existence, yet enjoyment of existence does not confer Existence. How then is Existence not superior to mere enjoyment of existence, since it is more one's own?

Secondly, although the soul of Christ sees all things in the Word and sees the Word himself in the

Word, yet because his soul is not admitted to the fellowship of Existence itself, neither can it be admitted to equality of knowledge. For who shall we say knows all the joy and delight of being God by nature and of being Wisdom and utmost Goodness and Excellence supreme and alone and everlasting, but the only One admitted to be all this by Essence? Hence the Word of the Father knows himself and all things through himself, the more intimately and clearly and simply, the more unity in the [divine] Essence is founded on a higher prerogative than unity in the [divine] Person.

4. We apply this difference to distinguish the excellences of the one Jesus Christ, in accordance with the twofold nature in Christ, that is, the excellences of the Word born of the Father by nature and those of his spirit created in time. This we do especially because of those who argue from the unity of person to equality or rather to unity of excellence and knowledge. Yet since they claim that his soul possesses by grace everything which the Word possesses by nature, they seem to introduce certain distances and degrees, if I may use these terms, by this distinction of names, that is, of nature and of grace. How much do they refuse him who do not concede that he possesses or knows the divine nature by nature?[7] For although the soul of Jesus, because united to the Word, is enlightened pre-eminently and by grace, shall his soul also be said to possess by grace the prerogative of being both light and the source of light, by nature and essence and without addition? Or in what way will the knowledge of nature excel that of grace, if it is not by clarity? But they adduce those words of Scripture and very true they are: 'All wisdom is from the Lord God and was with him always and was before all ages.'* If all wisdom is from God and with him, and that before all ages, how then are there many wisdoms together with the wisdom which is from God and is coeternal with him, because it is with him before all ages? There are then not many or various and different wisdoms, but one alone and invariable.

Ws 1:1.

5. This question is then no longer restricted to the one soul of the Lord Jesus, but extends to all souls which partake of any wisdom, so that it can be asked likewise whether all souls have one wisdom with the Word of God, or indeed whether all souls have any other wisdom than that which the very Word of God possesses. If this is so, then the wisdom of all souls will be one and undivided. And for what reason is it called 'all' wisdom, if there is only one wisdom?

What if wisdom is spoken of in the plural, not in itself it can be numbered, but on account of the numbers of those who possess it? Now faith also is spoken of as one, because of the one reality which is believed, although everyone has his own faith. Why then should one thing not be spoken of in the plural, when many things are spoken of in the singular? Again we speak of many acts of knowledge and of will in the same person and at the same time, on account of the number of things which even simultaneously he either knows or wills. Considering then the things known and not the power of the mind by which every person knows all he knows, we speak of the many acts of knowledge of one person and the one knowledge of many persons. Accordingly the text: 'All Wisdom is from the Lord God', is no obstacle to asserting the unity of wisdom, for the word 'all' refers not to wisdom but to the things which are known by it.

Now because many things are illumined in order that they may be seen, or that many people may be able to see, it does not follow that the light is multiple which illumines the things seen and shines upon those who see them. What then? Shall we say that the knowledge of the soul of Jesus is one and the same as the knowledge of the Word, indeed that there exists one wisdom of all rational spirits among themselves and with the Word of God, because the Word of God is Wisdom? At last then this discussion will no longer be concerned with the soul of Jesus alone and there will be no way for us to preserve the difference which we have asserted above between the knowledge of the Word and that of Jesus' soul.

And how can any way be found out of the difficulty, when the wisdom of all is thus proven to be
one, because the light which illumines all is one? Or
perhaps because the illumination takes place in
different ways, do the illuminations differ one from
another and differ from the light by which they are
caused? So also perhaps, in rational souls divinely illuminated, will both the light by which they are
illumined and the illumination which is caused by the
light, be distinguished from one another? For the
illumination, to be sure, is produced in the one
illumined and is produced in time, whereas the light
itself is not created but simply exists, and exists from
eternity. In this way who would deny that there are
many acts of knowledge in the one mind in which he
admits that there are many acts of comprehension,
although there exists only one power of the mind
which comprehends and sees and only one light which
illumines in order that the mind may be able to comprehend and see?

These therefore must be carefully distinguished:
the light and the illumination produced by the light
in the spirit of the one who understands. For this is
what it means to understand and to be illumined and
to know. Who then would not see (although because
of some similarity, the distinction may be made only
with great subtlety) who, I say, would not see that
the light by which the illumination is caused and the
illumination which is caused by the light in anyone
who is illumined, differ from each other? For the one
is created, the other creates; the one is illumined, the
other illuminates. Neither can the wisdom which
comes through grace be essentially the same as that
which exists by its nature, nor can that which is produced in time be the same as that which is born from
eternity.

6. If you have made these distinctions in your
Beloved, O bride, and if, from the powers which are
in him in accordance with the condition of his human
nature, you have passed on to the riches of the Word,
then with perfect right you can say: 'When I had

passed on a little beyond them, I found him whom
my soul loves'. But how shall we fit in the expression
'a little'? The divine majesty immeasurably transcends
every creature, yet as if the divine majesty were close
and familiar, the bride says: 'When I had passed on a
little beyond them, I found him whom my soul
loves'. In Scripture, a great gulf is fixed between
the divine nature and ours. What kind of gulf, you
ask. To be sure, that of our emptiness: 'All the
nations', says Isaiah, 'are as nought before him; as
nothing and emptiness he accounts them'.* Rightly is   *Is 40:17.*
our substance considered empty, for by assuming it
his fullness is said to have emptied itself.* What ap-   *Ph 2:7.*
proach then and what nearness can the void have with
what is solid, can nothingness have with what is immense? For what reason then does the bride say:
'When I had passed on a little beyond them, I found
him whom my soul loves'? Is it perhaps that charity
is winged and soars with the swift flight of ardent
desire over this intervening gulf of which we are
speaking? Yes, I agree. For to love is already to possess; to love is also to be assimilated and united. But
why not, since God is charity?*   *Jn 4:8.*

7. But I have another reason to add here. As one
moves upward from the contemplation of the highest
rational creature, immediately on the next level the
divine nature presents itself and appears; no other
intervening superior nature is discernible. For between the image and the reality can be found nothing
intermediate, which would both surpass the image
and yet be inferior to the reality. How can what is not
the original approach any nearer to the original than
by being its image and imprint? In a rational spirit,
then, in what way is the image thought to reflect the
divine nature? In the first place, by being capable of
truth and justice. Secondly, if the rational spirit, by
acquiring these virtues, becomes true and just by
grace, as God is by nature.

Here, in my view, three things are distinct:
namely to be capable of the supreme good, to possess the supreme good, and to be the supreme good.
The image is understood in the first, the likeness in

the second, the reality in the third. The first is common to all intelligent spirits; the second is reserved for the elect; the third belongs to the one uncreated Spirit. In the first we draw near, in the second very near; the third is God himself. We draw near by capability, very near by harmonious conformation;[8] near by the original endowments of our nature, very near by the prerogatives of virtue; near because able to receive, very near because actually receiving. For in what way does immortality not come close to immutability, incorporeity to simplicity, freedom from the limitations of place to immensity, reason to truth, virtue to goodness? And to speak more plainly, what can be closer and more like than wisdom to Wisdom, justice to Justice, an illumined soul to the One illuminating, a justified soul to the One justifying? What is more like something else than something caused to its cause, something formed to its form? For in what is formed, practically nothing is observed but the form. In scriptural terms, something sweet seems to be more than all else like sweetness and something illuminated like light. Accordingly, that rightly seems very near which consists in such a close imitation of the original, yes, very near, because nothing intervenes. For although our finitude is incomparably surpassed by the infinity of divine immensity, still some affinity of the image to the Original is discerned.

8. With good reason then the bride says: 'When I had passed on a little beyond them, I found him whom my soul loves'. Oh how happy, how joyous the outcome of such a long circuit! Blessed are the steps by which such a goal is reached. She sought him on her little bed, she made the rounds of the city, she questioned the watchmen. In the first place she seeks by herself and at home; in the second outside herself but by herself; in the third, however, neither by herself nor at home. And in this last the more humbly she seeks, the more effectively; the more she abandons her self-confidence, the sooner she finds him. 'I found him', she says, 'I found him', though previously he sought and found me like a stray sheep,

like a lost coin, and in his mercy anticipated me.*   *Mt 18:12; Lk 15:9; Ps 58:11.*

He forestalled me, I say, in finding me when I was lost. He anticipated me, though I deserved nothing. He found me astray, he anticipated me in my despair. He found me in my unlikeness, he anticipated me in my diffidence. He found me by pointing out my state to me, he anticipated me by recalling me to his own. He found me wandering in a labyrinth, he anticipated me with gifts when I was devoid of grace. He found me not that I might choose him but that he might choose me. He anticipated me that he might love me before I loved him.

In this way, then, chosen and loved, sought and acquired, found and anticipated, how should I not love and seek him with an effort according to my strength and with affection beyond my strength? I will seek him until gaining my desire I may utter my cry of happiness: 'I have found him whom my soul loves'. Personally, I ascribe the discovery here not to the beginning but to the increase of truth and grace. For as the soul advances and progresses from virtue to virtue, from truth to truth, as everywhere it is taught fresh mysteries and flooded with new joys, at each stage of its progress the soul can say: 'I have found him whom my soul loves', the Word of the Father, Christ Jesus who above all things is God blessed for ever and ever. Amen.[9]

NOTES TO SERMON EIGHT

1.   *Quaeris* in par. 6, is the only word of address.

2.   Reading *Denique haereticus, ne superiorem dilecto tuo gradum con-ferat, hunc tollit*; the *ne* of Mab., Migne and the Florentine ed. change to *ut*. 'The heresy of the Arians and of Apollinaris the Younger' is referred to here, Mab. For Apollinaris of Laodicea, see Karl Bihlmeyer, *Church History*, 1:268-69, with bibliography: 'The Arians not only denied the divinity of the Logos, they also mutilated His humanity by asserting that He inhabited a human body without a human soul . . . . When he [Apollinaris] was shown that such a doctrine was untenable according to Scripture, he restricted himself to teaching that Christ did not have the higher, intellectual soul (*psyche logike*) or mind (*nous*). As a Platonist he held the trichotomy of man. Hence he declared that Christ had assumed our flesh (*sarx*) and an animal soul (*psyche sarkike*) but that the Logos took the place of the higher soul or spirit.'

3.   Reading *claritatis* for *charitatis.*

4.   *Existendo,* and reading *fruendo* for *utendo.* See Miquel, pp. 158-59; his French translation of par. 2-3, differs from this version in several important points.

5.   Reading *permitteret* for *permittere.*

6.   Reading *participare* for *participle.*

7.   *Quantum illi denegant, qui hoc ipsum non dant per naturam habere vel nosse?*

8.   *Coaptationem* is Augustine's coinage for the Greek 'harmony' in *Trin.* 4:2, and *De civ. dei*, 22:24. See Bernard SC 80:2-6, 81:1-11.

9.   See Bernard SC 1:12; SBOp 2:93; PL 183:1031. This last par. summarizes the first eight sermons of G.

SERMON 9,
HOLDING FAST IN LOVE

The bride holds him fast by the labor of love.
1. How Abraham, Moses, Jacob, Magdalen, and
Simeon differ from the bride. 2. Who has the
happiness of finding and never losing Christ?
Not one bound by the habit of vice; 3. but one
clothed in Christ, to whom virtue has become
like second nature. 4. The fuller meaning of the
bride's words is fulfilled not here but in the
heavenly Jerusalem.

I HAVE TAKEN HOLD OF HIM AND I WILL NOT
LET HIM GO, UNTIL I BRING HIM INTO MY
MOTHER'S HOUSE, AND INTO THE CHAMBER
OF THE ONE WHO CONCEIVED ME[1] *

Sg 3:4.

'I have taken hold of him and I will not let him
go'. For my part I wished to interpret this verse
only of future happiness, when the Bridegroom
will show his beloved the full revelation of his
presence, that nothing might interrupt its continuity.
For the preceding words, 'when I had passed on a
little way beyond them', are aptly connected with
the text: 'When he has done away with every princi-
pality and power, . . . that God may be all in all'.*   *1 Co 15:24, 28.*
Before that time who can say with conviction: 'I will
not let him go'? Now to dislodge my interpretation,
the next verse follows closely and imposes a reference
to the present: 'Until I bring him into my mother's
house'.

Now let us carefully consider each point. First

reflect how full of joy are these words: 'I have found him, held him, and will not let him go'. The great patriarch Abraham is said to have seen the Lord, not to have found him. For the Lord appeared to him unasked as he stood at the door of his tent at midday. Then Abraham, emerging from the tent to meet him, beneath the spreading ilex showed him every mark of hospitality.* But Abraham was not found worthy to bring him into his tent, let alone into his chamber. Moses also saw the Lord who appeared to him on Horeb, but he was not found worthy to take hold of him nor was he allowed to draw near.* Jacob saw the Lord, but saw him in a dream, saw him from afar at the top of a ladder.* For although he took hold of the angel, he did not keep hold of him but wrung the favor of a blessing from him by dint of hard wrestling.* Then Jacob lost his presence and so could not say: 'I will not let him go'.

Mary of Magdala found him but she was forbidden not only to take hold of him but even to touch him,* because she looked for life near a tomb. The old man Simeon took him into his arms, long awaited and unexpectedly found, and broke into a joyful song of thanksgiving. But he did not presume to make his own these words: 'I will not let him go'. What he said was: 'Now you let your servant depart in peace, O Lord, in accordance with your word'.* Yes, in peace he is allowed to depart, set free and liberated from the flesh that it may no longer lust and do battle against his spirit. Simeon lays aside the decrepitude of an aging man for the embrace of a newborn child and either petitions or rejoices to be released from the burden of a corruptible body and from the battle against the flesh for a more peaceful state. But the bride assumes that her Beloved should not be released. Is it not a much greater grace to retain what you love than to escape what you abhor?

2. Although all these saw him in the flesh or in the appearance of the flesh, they illustrate differences between several levels either of vision or of comprehension in human minds. A privilege not ascribed to any of them, the bride claims in the words

Gn 18:1-8.

Ex 19 & 34.

Gn 28:12-13.

Gn 32:24-29.

Jo 20:16-17.

Lk 2:28-29.

we are trying to sift: 'I found him, I held him and I will not let him go'. 'I found him' by yearning for him, 'I held him' by dwelling on him in my memory, and 'I will not let go' by uninterrupted recollection. 'I held him.' When you also have found Christ, when you have found wisdom, when you have found justice, holiness and redemption (for Christ became all these for us),* when you have found all these, hold them by affection and by attention. What you have found by understanding, hold by diligence and keep hold, if I may so express it, of the elusive virtues. Clasp their slippery forms to you in a tighter embrace until, reversing their roles, they cling to you, embrace you willingly, hold you fast without the labor of your own initiative, and permit you neither to depart very far nor to be away very long.[2] Even if at times you should turn aside to meet the claims of human need, there let them pursue you, recall you, and clutch you to themselves, so that if they cannot always have your uninterrupted attention, they may always have your dedicated affection.

Now there seems to me to be a distinction between holding Christ, the excellence and wisdom of God, and your being held by him. Love wisdom, says the Proverb, and it will embrace you.* Then it is also said of some people, that 'pride has taken hold of them'.* What does 'taken hold' mean but ensnared and entangled and bound in the unbreakable chain of inveterate habit?[3] For this verse follows: 'They were covered with their iniquity and impiety',* so that they could not easily wriggle out and extricate themselves from that habit. Indeed those who are caught in the habit of vices, if I may amplify, are as it were covered and wrapped in a hide, so that to unlearn and break the habit is not so much to be stripped as to be flayed.[4] Perhaps as evidence of this, the prescriptions of the Law ordain that a victim's hide is to be stripped off.*

3. Now the directive which commands a priest to be vested in binding linen* requires you to be more tightly bound in the habit of that Truth which 'has arisen from the earth',* in order that by itself the

1 Co 1:30.

Pr 4:5-8.

Ps 72:6.

Ps 72:8.

Lv 1:6.

Ex 28:4; Lv 8:8.

Ps 84:12.

Ex 28:14, 28:39;
28:28.
†Rm 13:14.

Col 3:12.

Ps 72:24; see
Lam p. 199,
n. 190.

Ps 118:20.

virtue of chastity, purity and innocense may cling to
you and stick fast to you. The Law requires no less
that all priestly vestments be fastened and gathered in
by little chains or belts or ribbons,* that when you
have put on our Lord Jesus Christ,† when you have
put on 'the bowels of his compassion, kindness,
charity' and the other virtues of which you read in
Paul,* when in your memory you have been clothed
with faith in Christ and have filled your marrow with
a yearning for the contemplation of truth, everything may fit and cling and be bound to you, and
nothing can float and wave and flap around you, as if
blown in the wind of temptation or dissipation.

Of the man clad in such a habit of virtue that for
him virtue seems to have become second nature, I
would say that he has not so much embraced as been
embraced by virtue. 'You have taken hold of my
right hand', says the psalmist, 'and you have guided
me with your counsel'.* 'You have taken hold' lest
I hasten towards a fall; 'you have guided me' to manifold progress; 'you have guided me with your counsel', that is, with counsel which is from you and
follows you, with counsel which attracts rather than
is attracted. For at times we strive with great effort
to attract even good counsel and we pursue it like a
fugitive rather than follow it as a leader. For so the
psalmist says: I have longed to desire.* Good is that
counsel but not yet pleasant, correct but not yet
agreeable. 'In your counsel you have guided me', in
that counsel which depends on the alluring taste of
goodness itself and relies, if I may so express it, not
so much on sluggish reason as on a holy delight in
goodness itself.

4. 'I have taken hold of him and I will not let him
go, until I have brought him into my mother's house
and into the chamber of the one who conceived me.'
There would seem to be a much fuller meaning,[5] if
she had said: 'I will not let him go when I have
brought him into the house of my mother, that is, of
the heavenly Jerusalem which is above, who is the
mother of us all. Before that time all things here are
unreliable; they fluctuate between hope and fear

and hang in the balance. And what is our assurance of
grace, when nature is fickle? Again the psalmist says:
'As for me, I said in my prosperity: "I shall never be
moved". You hid your face from me and I was put to
confusion'.* Do you not think that the psalmist and   *Ps 29:7-8.*
the bride said much the same thing? What else is
the meaning of: 'I shall never be moved', but what
we are now considering: 'I will not let him go'? Yet in
the former text his presumption is obvious, because
retribution is close at hand: 'You hid your face from
me and I was put to confusion'.

Because in this mortal flesh, alas, a fall is easy,
attacks are frequent, lapses come quickly and toil is
inevitable, how shall these words of the bride, 'I will
not let him go', not seem to proceed from presumption and an impetuous devotion? Who on earth will be
able to persevere in the same state, especially in that
state of most subtle contemplation which can scarcely
be attained by the most delicate thrust of the mind?
Perhaps then her words show not her self-assurance
but her anxiety. For there cannot be any assurance
until she has brought her Beloved 'into her mother's
house and into the chamber of the one who conceived her'. Then there will be no anxiety about
keeping him, because there will be certainty about
remaining in that state of bliss. Without our need for
attention and our safeguard of discipline, streams of
living water and of unwearying delight will flow over
us unbidden. Indeed they will surge within us from
an inexhaustible well of the soul. Then there will be
no need to dig deep, no labor to clear the wells which
the Philistines have polluted,* no expedition to pre-   *Gn 26:18.*
vent their pollution of the wells. Here that labor is
demanded, for there it is excluded. So the bride's
resolve, 'I will not let him go', seems to promise both
attention and diligence, that she may be ever solici-
tous until she can be fully secure, lest in future her
Beloved should slip away from her, the Lord Jesus
who lives and reigns for ever and ever. Amen.

NOTES TO SERMON NINE

1.   This sermon addresses one individual. This verse is a refrain; see Bernard SC 52 on Sg 2:7, and John of Ford, Sermons 98-99 on Sg 5:2-8.

2.   Seems to refer to Menelaus wrestling with Proteus, Homer, *The Odyssey*, 4:450-70.

3.   Reading *indissolubili* rather than *delicato*.

4.   May refer to the flayed seal-skins in Homer, *The Odyssey*, 4:435-40, or to Marsyas, the satyr flayed alive by Apollo.

5.   Reading *multo plenior sensus* with Mab. rather than *planior* with Migne.

SERMON 10,
HOLDING AND BEHOLDING

The lover holds and beholds him, steadfast in charity. 1. Charity calls from contemplation to action, but works of charity are a prayer. 2. Active and contemplative life differ. 3. The virtues are gradually acquired. 4. The first finding and holding of Christ is not the final possession.

I WILL NOT LET HIM GO, UNTIL I HAVE BROUGHT HIM INTO MY MOTHER'S HOUSE[1]*   *Sg 3:4.*

In the preceding sermon we contrasted with the bride examples of weakness; today let us compare examples of strength from sacred Scripture. Of Hannah it is said that when she prayed earnestly with tearful affection, 'her countenance was no longer changed into something different'.*   *1 S 1:18.* The countenance is the interpreter of the spirit and derives its expression from inmost affection. Steadfastness of countenance is evidence of an inner perseverance which exists in the soul. Hannah's countenance was no longer changed, because there was no lessening of the longing she had once conceived. What else does the bride mean when she says 'I will not let him go', but that 'I will not change my countenance into something different' and I will not turn the gaze of my mind away from him'. The exhortation of Paul is similar: 'Pray without ceasing',*   *1 Th 5:17.* 'always giving thanks'*   **Ep 5:20.* and 'rejoicing in the Lord always'†.   *†Ph 4:4.* Paul wants prayer, thanksgiving and joy in the Lord to be

133

continuous and uninterrupted.

Yet who is competent to satisfy Paul's wish by the bent of his mind and his unwearied affection of spirit, but a man permitted to say: who shall separate us from the contemplation of Christ? Paul does say: 'Who shall separate us from the love of Christ'?* He could not say 'from the contemplation of Christ'. Yes, at times charity compelled him to be removed from the contemplation of Christ. 'If we were out of our mind, it was for God', he said, 'and if we are in our right mind, it is for you, for the love of Christ impels us'.* Charity then, by a kind of dispensation, withdraws from contemplation, although the practice of contemplation is proper and familiar to charity. All good works of charity have their opportunity and effectiveness from tireless prayer and thanksgiving. But charity performs good works more freely and more perfectly when it is engaged in good works in a special way. Slip alms unseen into the bosom of the poor man and 'alms will pray for you to the Lord'.[2]

In the word 'alms' may appropriately be included everything given with compassion to the needy, not only food and clothing for the body, but also teaching, exhortation, correction, consolation, and everything which seems to concern only the well-being of the soul. The latter are works of charity and are invested with the power of prayer when performed with God alone in mind, though they are not the special and characteristic works of charity. For what is so characteristic of charity as to wait upon the Beloved alone and to engage freely in the commerce of love? To return to sobriety after this transport and inebriation of spiritual pleasure and for a brother's needs to refrain from ecstasy, what is this but to 'change one's countenance into something different'? Martha also was 'anxious and troubled about many things'. That trouble about many things resembles some 'change of countenance into something different'. 'Mary has chosen the best role, which will not be taken away from her'.*

2. The best role is the practice of contemplation

Rm 8:38.

2 Co 5:13-14.

Lk 10:41-42.

and love. For although the works which Martha was performing are works of charity, nonetheless charity there is the handmaid of necessity, not its own handmaid. To relieve the needs of others is indeed a good work but the reason for it is disturbing. Indeed compassion is good, but wretchedness disturbing. Healing is good, but the illness about which it is concerned is not good. The feeling of compassion in necessity is good, but the suffering of another which provides the occasion for compassion is not good. In the needs of the brethren, charity looks for someone with whom to grieve and to be moved to compassion, and something to try to remedy. But when the virtues of the Beloved are contemplated, everything pleases, everything delights, everything attracts. Charity there sees nothing loathesome to face but only what it may gently embrace.

This is the proper practice of love, this is its duty: to be wholly immersed in loving. So love clearly exists when one and the same delight enfolds and embraces all three: duty and cause and end. The duty is love, the cause is vision, the end is both; there cannot be any more blessed end than the very vision and love of God. All the longings of the saints aspire to this end. This end is an end in itself, content with itself, incapable of directing its expectations to anything better. This is the one thing said to be necessary, which is not taken away from Mary and in which the psalmist rejoices: 'For me it is good to cling to God'.*   *Ps 72:28.*

This is the transport of mind which had swept Paul even to the third heaven.*   *2 Co 12:2.* This is the inebriation which made Hannah's countenance beam like that of a tippler.*   *1 S 1:13.* With this ferment the apostles were intoxicated, when the mighty spirit had filled them*   *Ac 2:1-21.* and they felt for the first time the might of wine which Jesus promised as something new.*   *Mt 26:29.* Brimful of this wine, Noah underwent a transport of spiritual sleep and neglected the care of his person;*   *Gn 9:21.* made whole in spirit, he despised what lay behind, because what lay ahead wholly preoccupied him. Happy would he be if, like Hannah, he had never experienced the potency of wine from our grapes. In her body outwardly temperate, Hannah underwent a tipsiness of mind and a holy inebriation which subsequently she would not shake off. This is the meaning of the text that her 'countenance was not further changed into something different'.

Such a continuing awareness of her Beloved's presence the bride seems to promise herself, when she says 'I will not let him go'. For would she be saying anything distinguished, anything spiritual, anything worthy of a bride, if her statement, 'I will not let him go', referred to faith, justice, humility, continence, generosity and the other virtues which Christ is said to be? It is incredible that she should lack these virtues, even when she was seeking her Beloved. In Scripture, virtues such as these are ordinary and so suitable for those who possess them, that it would be considered impious to lack them.

3. Therefore her discovery indicates something extraordinary and uncommon, whereby she boasts that she has caught her Beloved and assumes that he is not to be released. Perhaps these are some firstfruits of future contemplation and glory; therefore she adds 'until I bring him into my mother's house, into the chamber of her who conceived me', into that heavenly Jerusalem who is mother of us all, whose walls are the dwelling of Salvation, whose gates are the haunt of praise, and whose boundaries are marked for peace.* Into that place of light and rejoicing, the laborious virtues of this life cannot be introduced; if they enter by merit, they are locked out by their need for exercise. Having experienced then in her Beloved, a heavenly affection and an otherworldly savor, the bride adds not as a boast but in jubilation:* 'I will not let him go, until I bring him into my mother's house'.

But has he not already ascended to his Father? Has he not entered on our behalf, our precursor? And how will you introduce him there, where he has ascended before you? Rather you need him to lead you, for to him the Psalmist says: 'Lead me in the way of your commandments'.* 'I am going away' he

Is 60:18, 17.

Miquel, p. 157, n. 26.

*Ps 118:35;
G: in via; Vulg.:
in semitam.*

says, 'to prepare a place for you'; when I have done so, 'I will come again and take you to myself'.* *Jn 14:2-3.* How then will you introduce him there, where he has already ascended? He has ascended indeed in himself, but in you he still stands outside; in you he is introduced there, where in his own person he ascended before you. But why not? He is born in you, he is formed in you. Is he not also introduced in you? 'Little children', says Paul, 'with whom I am again in travail, until Christ be formed in you'.* *Ga 4:19.* Christ then is born and made perfect in us, not once but often, and I believe by a travail often and frequently repeated. Neither can we make all Christ's virtues our own at the same time nor fully reproduce even one virtue. Therefore we must persevere at all times, for only gradually does the spiritual birth of Christ take place in us.

Since then in his members he is born in his bride, why is he not introduced in her? For neither this birth nor this introduction of Christ can be applied to Christ's person but to his virtues and to his grace. Therefore as the birth, so the introduction is often repeated. Now we are also said to be seated in heavenly places together with Christ.* But as there is *Ep 2:6.* one, true and eternal session in heaven, so also there is a like introduction. Abraham walked through the land of promise before he came into possession of it.* Happy indeed is the one who is allowed to walk *Gn 12-17.* through those blessed regions and like a visitor to tread with quick step every place which he is to receive into his possession. Happy is one who, though not permitted to linger, is allowed to ascend the mountain of the Lord and, although in shadow still and for a brief moment, to scan the whole horizon and be regaled with such a view.

4. But the true and complete introduction seems to be suggested here by the words: 'until I bring him into my mother's house'. Happy indeed is she who was able to bind and closely bond the Word of God to herself and in exile to keep him at her side until she is allowed to be united with him in this chamber. 'I will not let him go until I bring him into my

mother's house and into the chamber of her who
conceived me'. This will happen when in body and
mind she will bear fully the likeness of the heavenly
one, since you may interpret the house to mean the
body and the chamber to mean the mind. Or, if you
prefer, take the house to mean assured possession,
the chamber to mean secret possession; the house
everlasting possession, the chamber interior posses-
Qo 12:5.   sion; the house, as Ecclesiastes says,* possession of
eternity, and the chamber possession of charity. In
the chamber, where you may no longer pray to the
Father behind closed doors, for the future you may
Jo 4:23.   still adore him 'in spirit and truth'.* 'Into the
house', she says, not of my father but 'of my mother'
and 'into the chamber of her who conceived me'.
She knows the measure allotted to her and therefore
she extends her hope to that eternity, truth and
charity which the Church of the firstborn has
attained in heaven.⁵ Now considering what belongs
to God, he alone possesses immortality and 'dwells in
1 Tm 6:16.   unapproachable light',* while the fullness of Christ's
charity surpasses all knowledge. May he fill us to utter
Ep 3:19.   fullness in himself,* who is the blessed God and reigns
for ever and ever. Amen.

NOTES TO SERMON TEN

1.   The sermon addresses one individual.
2.   Si 29:15; G: *absconde . . . sinu*; Vulg.: *conclude corde*. See Lam. p. 192, n. 148.
3.   *Ecclesia primitivorum in coelis.* See also S 13:3, 34:1, 38:4, 41:1, 45:7. See G. Olsen, 'The Idea of the *Ecclesia primitiva* in the writings of the Twelfth-Century Canonists', in *Trad.* 25 (1969) 61-86; E. T. Kennan, 'The *De consideratione* of S. Bernard of Clairvaux and the Papacy in the mid-twelfth century: A Review of Scholarship', in Trad. 23 (1967) 87ff. 'As Olsen shows, the "ecclesia primitiva" is the symbol of the perfect life both for monks and for clerics. The words of the *Exordium Magnum,* "scola primitivae ecclesiae", are typical. The expression "ecclesia primitiva" became so current as signifying a model of religious life that at times it became a label giving a historical guarantee to institutions alleged to have existed in the early Church'. Cyprian Davis in *Bulletin of Monastic Spirituality* 1970-72, no. 593.

SERMON 11,
KEEPING SABBATH FREE

The bride keeps sabbath free to see him.
1. Love frets over distractions; 2. contempla-
tion surpasses activities; 3. and is compared to a
Sabbath, the Sabbath of the Lord after Crea-
tion and after the Restoration. 4. Contempla-
tion is freedom from outer works for inner life.
5. Do not waste this leisure, this triple freedom.

I HAVE TAKEN HOLD OF HIM AND I WILL NOT
LET HIM GO UNTIL I BRING HIM INTO MY
MOTHER'S HOUSE AND INTO THE CHAMBER
OF HER WHO CONCEIVED ME[1] *   *Sg 3:4.*

T he affection of love is a delicate plant and
spiritual joy is wounded by the slightest
mishap. Love frets over outward occupations, considering it enough to mind its
own business. Love rejoices in leisure and is encouraged by repose. Love longs to have periods free
for interior delights.[2] Do you not think the bride
implies this, when she draws her Beloved into the
privacy of the chamber? She knows that, outside, her
Beloved cannot be securely or even wholly possessed.
And how hard it is for a lover to divide the spirit
between Christ and the world! How hard it is, I say,
to admit alien cares to the rights of perfect love and
to disturb the heavenly mystery with throngs of
worldlings. 'I was mindful of God', says the psalmist,
'and I was delighted, but I was drained and my
spirit grew faint'.* If delight drains itself and exhausts   *Ps ·76:4.*

141

the prophet's spirit in the business of remembering God, how can many and alien affairs be embraced along with God? Rightly then does the bride seek the chamber with her Beloved, that she may wait upon him with unhampered attention, enjoy him with freedom of spirit and embrace him utterly with peace of heart. Clearly she who seeks in this way an opportunity of engaging in love is led by the spirit of charity and has spoken with the affection of a bride.

2. If we have made some slight approach to Christ, to wisdom, to sweetness, to the taste of contemplation, how is it that, not satisfied with that grace and disregarding our limitations, we at once struggle to break out and, disdaining our cells, hasten to abandon our rest, a rest so great? 'In peace', says the psalmist, 'in the self-same, I will sleep and take my rest'.* Seated at the Lord's feet, Mary held fast to that 'self-same', while Martha was troubled about many things. In many things there is trouble, but 'one thing is necessary'* and indeed pleasant. Then 'how good and how pleasant it is', when lovers 'dwell together in unity!'*[3] There is no dwelling together in unity, except in a love, 'which causes those sharing a common outlook to live together in the same house'.* What does 'sharing a common outlook' mean but sharing one form through the covenant of love? Love reconciles and unites the human spirit with God. 'We shall be like him', says John, 'when he appears'.*

Ps 4:9; in pace in idipsum dormiam et requiescam.

Lk 10:39-42.

Ps 132:1.

Ps 67:7.

1 Jn 3:2.

Why should we not be like him? The inestimable beauty of the divine majesty, once revealed, commends itself to pure minds, ravishes the affection of the beholder, and in some way makes the mind like itself, allowing it to think of nothing else. We are lured by scent but we are transformed by sight. Good then is the practice of contemplation, which confers upon the human mind a common outlook and brings it into conformity with the supreme Majesty. Good it is to dwell here, for desires lure us no further and desires should not stop our advancing so far. Who will grant that this may be my rest for ever and ever? Happy the man who can say from his heart: 'This is my dwelling, for I have chosen it'.* Mary has chosen the best part, which shall not be taken away from her.* Knowledge will pass, prophecies will disappear, tongues will cease;* contemplation alone will not fail in the future. Therefore choose this part for yourself for the present, for this part will never be taken away, that your soul may say: 'The Lord is my part' and therefore I shall contemplate him. The prophet says: 'Therefore I shall look for him'.* And rightly, because he looks for the fullness of goodness, a portion of which he already possesses. One who here enjoys the good of contemplation may look for something more of the same kind, but ought not to look for something different.

3.   These good things are blessings stored up for many years, indeed for years · without end. Happy then are you, O soul, if you enjoy this good; dine, feast, for your portion will not be taken away, but [will be] more bountifully renewed and reformed. This is your rest for ever and ever; 'This is my dwelling, for I have chosen it'.* Dwell here, that you may dwell with him who sits above the Cherubim,* above the fullness of knowledge, who 'dwells in light inaccessible'.* So let your place be in the light of contemplation. This is the proper and familiar place of your mother the Church, this is her house; other duties, which she carries out to meet temporal needs, look to this end. Duties of the active life are transient; those of the contemplative life are permanent. It is good for you to be here; here build a tabernacle for yourself, not one for yourself and another for your Beloved but one for the two of you.*

Introduce your Beloved into this chamber. Enter into your repose, that you may rest from your labors, as God did from his. On the seventh day he rested from the work of creation; on the seventh day he rested from the work of restoration. On the former day, after he established the universe; on the latter, when he hid himself in the tomb. On the former day, after setting the universe on its foundation; on the latter, after renewing mankind. If you have sought, if you have found, if you have taken

Ps 131:14. See Lam, p. 8, n. 21.

Lk 10:42.

1 Co 13:8.

Lm 3:24. .

Ps 131:14.

Is 37:16.

1 Tm 6:16.

Mt 17:4. See Lam, p. 6, n. 4.

hold‛ of your Beloved, hold fast the one you hold.
Hold fast, cling to him, press yourself upon him,
that his image, expressed as it were in you, may
be renewed, that you may be the imprint of his seal.*
But this you will be, if you cling to him, 'for the man
who clings to God is one spirit with him'.* Perhaps it
is difficult at first to imprint him upon yourself as
upon hard metal. But if the imprinting is laborious,
the clinging is sweet. Laborious is the sixth day of
your reformation, but sweet are the sabbaths of rest
which follow.[4]

4. Be buried then together with Christ, by keeping this sabbath unto death.* For 'blessed are the
dead who die in the Lord; from now on, says the
Spirit, they may rest from their labors'.* The Spirit
says this by revealing and bringing about the repose
and grace already conferred, just as the 'Spirit himself bears witness to our spirit'.* The Spirit says this,
because the Spirit brings this about. The Spirit says
this, because he grants this. 'From now on, says the
Spirit, they may rest from their labors'. 'From their
labors', he says, not 'from their works', for their
works follow them'.* Works follow the spirit as heat
follows fire, shadow a body, light the sun, an effect
its cause. He who keeps sabbath in the Spirit has no
need to pursue works, for his works follow him.

'Their works.' What are their works? What are the
works of those at rest, the works of those who have
died in Christ and been buried with Christ, the works
of those keeping sabbath? They are festive works,
holiday works; they are works equivalent to leisure.[5]
Hasten to enter into this rest, into this holding of sabbath. But note that celebrating a sabbath is left only
for those who are buried with Christ, only after the
sixth day, that day on which either the old man is
crucified or the new man is perfected. For because of
the Sabbath after the crucifixion, one is told how
those who have died in Christ rest from their labors.
Because of the sabbath after the creation, when the
new man had been created on the sixth day, one is
told that God rested from his works on the seventh.*
Do you also secure a sabbath for yourself, redeem

Marginal references (left column):

Cf. 2 Co 3:18;
Rm 8:29.

1 Cor 6:17.

Rm 6:4. See Lam,
p. 10, n. 28.

Rv 14:13.

Rm 6:8.

Rv 14:13.

Gen 2:2.

your time,* and claim for yourself hours free
from outward occupation.

5. But take care lest enemies mock your sabbaths, lest your times of leisure serve them, lest you
be free for them, when you should have been free for
God. 'Be free and see that I am God',* says the
psalmist. Leisure is good, but 'write of wisdom in
your time to leisure'.*[6] Write wisdom on the breadth
of your heart. For the heart is broad which is not
shrivelled by cares. Imprint in the depth of your
heart letters which are indelible, and inscribe characters of wisdom on the tablets of your spirit, that you
may be able to say: 'The light of your countenance
was stamped upon us, O Lord; you have put gladness
into my heart'.* Rejoice and keep holiday with your
Beloved, feasting, as it is written, at the entrance of
such glory.* 'The sabbath', as Isaiah says,† 'is the
delightful and holy and glorious day of the Lord.'[7]
'Delightful and holy', he says.

Everyone at leisure is full of desires,* but not all
desires are holy; witness those of the men 'who wish
to become rich' and thereby 'fall into many useless
and harmful desires'.* You see how Paul counts as a
vice a multitude of desires. What if these desires are
also unclean? Many who are unable to carry out their
desires think in secret of what would be indecent
even to mention, finding satisfaction in this vain
subterfuge. To exclude such persons, not content to
call the sabbath 'delightful', Isaiah adds, 'and the
holy and glorious day of the Lord', that your glory
may not be to your shame. If you are free, you have a
sabbath; if you are free and have eyes to contemplate
the delights of the Lord, then your sabbath is
'delightful and holy', a glorious sabbath of the
Lord; a sabbath within a sabbath, that is freedom
in freedom.[8]

The first freedom is good, if you are not free for
the world. The second indeed is better, if you are
free for yourself and think of how you may please
God.* The third is the best, if, forgetful even of
yourself, you are free only for God and think of
what concerns the Lord, how he may be pleasing to

Eph 5:16.

Ps 45:11.

Si 38:25.

Ps 4:7.

**Ps 75:11;
Lk 15:23.*

†Is 58:13.

Pr 21:25.

1 Tm 6:9.

1 Co 7:32.

you. Let not your sabbath be one of idleness; perform the works of God on your sabbath. Now the work of God is that you should believe in him. It is by faith that you see. Indeed we see now in a mirror;* therefore be free, that you may see. Sight, and especially the sight of God, is a delightful work. For the future, there is no necessity for you to fight for the faith but only to take your delight in the faith. The faith has already been snatched from the attacks of the people who persecuted it and of the heretics who distorted it. Let faith head the column of your thoughts, that you may think the 'trustworthy thoughts of old. Amen'.*[9]

1 Co 13:12.

Is 25:1.

NOTES TO SERMON ELEVEN

1.   The sermon is addressed to one individual.
2.   Cited by Leclercq, *Otia Monastica,* SAn 51 (1963) 90:31.
3.   G: *amantes,* Vulg.: *fratres*; see Lam p. 15, n. 55.
4.   Leclercq, *Otia Monastica,* 105:7.
5.   Leclercq, *Otia Monastica,* 105:14.
6.   Vulg.: *vacuitatis,* G: *otii.*
7.   G. writes *delicatum est et sanctum et Domini gloriosum,* Mab.
8.   Leclercq, *Otia Monastica,* 119:23.
9.   The 'Amen' is within the quotation, but seems to have suggested to editors the end of the Sermon. Mabillon notes that in the Codex of Clairvaux, sermons eleven and twelve are not divided. The first manuscript to divide sermons eleven and twelve (Troyes, Bibliotheque Municipale, ms. 410, ff. 1-119) dates from the thirteenth century and also comes from Clairvaux.

SERMON 12,
BETWEEN HIS SHOULDERS AND HIS BREAST

The bride rests between his shoulders and on his breast. 1. Her rest demands an equipoise of law and liberty. 2. Outward repose is the opportunity for inward vision; 3. an opportunity for the joy, peace and sleep of contemplation. 4. What is the difference between contemplation upon his breast and between his shoulders?

I HAVE TAKEN HOLD OF HIM AND I WILL NOT LET HIM GO UNTIL I HAVE BROUGHT HIM INTO MY MOTHER'S HOUSE*[1]

Sg 3:4.

They know not how to entertain 'the thoughts of old',* who coin novelties in words,* who forge new dogmas, who do not reject puerile longings,* who have no ore stamped with gravity or authority or antiquity. There is no final 'Amen'* where there is dispute or deceit in thoughts, where either disbelief exists or faith wavers. Enter into the secure depths of faith. Introduce your Beloved into your mother's chamber, so that whatever experience, whatever opinion you have about Christ, you may keep within the rules of the Church and conform to her censure. Such works as these perform on your sabbath. Otherwise, if you are free and do not apply yourself to such pursuits, vain thoughts and poisoned counsels will easily sprout in an unharrowed spirit.[2] As you know from Proverbs, the field of the idler is overgrown with

Is 25:1.
1 Tm 6:20.
2 Tm 2:22.

Is 25:1.

149

Pr 24:30-31.

Lk 17:34.

*RB 5:10-12; see
Lam p. 8, n. 22;
p. 10, nn. 29, 33.*

nettles and thorns,* and in Luke the Lord tells you that 'there will be two in one bed; one will be taken and the other left'.* Like a bed is the life of leisure and repose for those who dwell in the bosom of the Church, not burdened with any ecclesiastical responsibility or distraught by solicitude for providing and distributing, but enjoying free leisure under the rule of another.* Yet not all use this leisure with an equipoise of law and liberty; but some turn the free time they gain into an occasion for idleness.[3]

2. Good is the bed if one uses it lawfully and turns an opportunity for outward repose into the enjoyment of inward vision. These are the ones who will be taken up from this chamber of the Church to the chamber of heaven, that where Christ is, there also they may be with him. According to Matthew: 'wherever the body shall be, there the eagles will gather'.* You, too, be like the eagle and use sharp eyes, grow accustomed to spiritual contemplation, perch in the rocks and linger on sheer cliffs of flint, or rather enter the caverns of that unique rock which is Christ.[5] 'Go into your rooms', as Isaiah says, 'shut your doors, . . . hide yourselves a little while until the wrath is past'.* Or rather hide forever, that your delight may last forever. Enter the chamber of peace, the mighty works of the Lord,* for peace exists in his might.* Be mindful 'of his justice alone',* that 'peace and justice' may meet together in you.* Be mindful 'of his justice alone', 'for what do you have that you have not received'?* 'His justice alone.' Good is the justice which you defend by combat against the vices tilting against you. More blessed is justice when you do not battle for it but rather take delight in it, when you are intent not on combat but on delight, when you are not wrestling with vices but embracing virtue. If you are clinging to virtue, you are not battling vice. When you forget the past, you do not 'think the thoughts' of men but those of God and you are mindful 'of his justice alone', since 'justice and peace have kissed each other' within you.* For 'the kingdom of God is justice and peace and joy'.* If such is the kingdom,

Mt 24:28.

Is 26:20.

Ps 70:15.

Ps 121:7.

Ps 70:16.

Ps 84:11.

1 Co 4:7.

Ps 84:11.

Rm 14:17.

why not also the house and the chamber? Indeed
'his place is in peace and his dwelling in Sion'.*   *Ps 75:3.*
Enter the chamber of peace, of this outward peace
yes, but even more of that inner peace, the dwelling
of contemplation, for Sion means contemplation. 'In
peace in the self-same, I will sleep and take my
rest.'* Interpret this 'self-same'† as contemplation,   *Ps 4:9.*
for this is the best role, which will not be taken   *†idipsum*
away. The bride in the Canticle also fell asleep with
her Beloved in the chamber of her mother and
experienced some transport of a mind slumbering in
the embrace of the Bridegroom. Hence follows the
verse: 'I adjure you . . . ' and so forth.*   *Sg 3:5.*

3. If you also have taken hold of the Bridegroom,
then hold him fast and do not release him until you
introduce him into the house and the chamber of
your mother. Why do I now urge you towards that to
which your own experience of past sweetness invites
and allures you more cogently? If anyone in a holiday spirit has, secretly and as if in rapture, been
enabled to foretaste the festive joys of unimpeded
meditation, I do not know whether such a one will
ever do anything more readily than surrender and
become wholly and entirely free for this pursuit.[6]
In our text, the first charms of fair contemplation
allured and enticed the bride into the chamber of
repose, where she exults in happiness at the prospect
of introducing her Beloved. 'I will not let him go,
until I bring him in.' Does she not seem to you to
echo in her words those of the psalm: 'I will give my
eyes no sleep, my eyelids no slumber . . . until I find
a place for the Lord'?* All else I abandon, lest I   *Ps 131:4-5.*
abandon him. I count everything as loss 'to gain
Christ',* because of the surpassing joy of his   *Ph 3:8.*
presence. 'If two sleep together they will keep each
other warm, but how shall one keep warm alone?'*   *Qo 4:11.*
This verse is in Ecclesiastes. Good it is to be kept
warm and inflamed in the embrace of the Word,
for the Word of the Lord is a blazing fire;* and good   *Ps 118:140.*
it is to burn with spiritual desires. Therefore 'I will
give my eyes no sleep, my eyelids no slumber', 'until
I bring him into my mother's chamber'.

Ph 3:24.   Then I shall rest and my sleep will be sweet.*
John slept, as it were, reclining upon the breast of
Jesus, where are stored 'all the treasures of the
wisdom and knowledge' of God.[7] There is the place
of true repose, the calm of understanding, the
sanctuary of piety, the chamber of delight. Sleep
here that you may see what John saw, the Word in the
beginning, the Word with God and the Word who
Jn 1:1.   was God,* and may understand in Christ coeternity
with the Father, distinction of person and unity in
nature. What seems to you more like sleep? Here
human gaze cannot penetrate, human reason cannot
intrude. According to Scripture, man shall not see
Ex 33:20.   these realities and live.* It is good then that you
should fell asleep and be lulled to forgetfulness of
human feelings and affections, that you be enabled
to dream such dreams. This is the chamber of the
apostles who begot us in Christ. Paul is like a mother
when he says: 'My little children, with whom I am
in labor until Christ be formed in you'.[8] The
'mother' then you know; would you know the
'chamber' also? 'Our homeland is in heaven', says
Ph 3:20.   Paul.* Would you know 'sleep' too? 'If we were out
2 Co 5:13.   of our mind, it was for God.'*

4. Make your way hither then with the Beloved,
remain here, ponder on these truths, dwell upon
them. Of if you cannot advance so far, act more
modestly. If you cannot recline on his breast where
the well of unwearied wisdom exists, rest between his
shoulders where you may contemplate the examples
and the mysteries of his suffering. Between his
shoulders, because 'dominion has been laid on his
Is 9:6.   shoulders'.* Of Benjamin also it was said that 'the
most beloved of the Lord . . . will rest between his
shoulders'. Jesus did indeed rest and fall asleep on
the cross, that you might sleep with him in your
belief and remembrance of his Passion. Or by preference pass from one to the other, from his breast to
his shoulders, from the mysteries of faith to the mani-
festation of truth. In the one build a home for yourself, in the other a chamber. 'The most beloved of the
Lord', Benjamin, 'will tarry all day as if in his

chamber and rest between his shoulders.'*   *Dt 33:12.*

Do you see how he places his chamber between
his shoulders? What then will be upon his breast?
Upon both clearly is the place of fair contemplation,
both between his shoulders and between his breasts.
But there is more fruitful grace upon his breast: the
place of love, the throne of thought, the chançe of
embrace and the freedom to behold his countenance.
Well placed then in the breast of Jesus is the bridal
chamber, indeed his treasury. There indeed are both
the delights of the Bridegroom and the wealth of the
Word, for in him 'have been hidden all the treasures
of the wisdom and knowledge' of God.* Enter into   *Col. 2:3.*
this treasury, hide yourself in the secret of his
countenance from the turmoil of men,* and let no   *Ps 30:21.*
one arouse or waken you until you yourself are
willing.* This also is implied in the following adjura-   *Sg 3:5.·*
tion of the Bridegroom, Christ Jesus who lives and
reigns for ever and ever. Amen.

NOTES TO SERMON TWELVE

1.   In the *Codex Vallis-Clarae* and in Flor., sermons eleven and twelve are continuous, both addressed to one individual. The 'Amen' which ended the quotation from Is 21:5, was taken to be the end of a sermon; see S 11, n. 9.

2.   Cited by Leclercq, *Otia Monastica*, 93:50.

3.   Reading *torporis* for *temporis,* with Mab. and Flor. See Lam, p. 20, n. 87.

5.   1 Co 10:4; Jb 28:27-30. Morson, p. 160; White, p. 105-7.

6.   Miquel, p. 151, n. 3; Lam, p. 185, n. 98.

7.   Col 2:3. See Leclercq, *Otia Monastica*, 121:34.

8.   Ga 4:19. See the prayer of St Anselm (1033-1109) to St Paul and to the Lord Jesus, as Mothers, in *Prayers and Meditations of Saint Anselm,* trans. by Benedicta Ward, SLG with foreword by R. W. Southern, (Harmondsworth: Penguin, 1973) pp. 141-156. See also Andre Cabussut, 'Une devotion peu connue', RAM 25 (1949) 234-45.

*Bound by charity, the bride endures the lash
and the crises. 1. We should not fear his
desertion but our defection. 2. The early
Church weathered the assault of the Synagogue;
3. and the attacks of persecutors; 4. until after
heresies, she brought Christ from the field of
battle into the chamber of peace. 5. The truth
of faith and the freedom of witness may be
lost by lack of love. 6. The present persecution
in the Church is an attack on morality. 7. Faith
dies in the Church and in the individual without
works of charity.*

I HAVE TAKEN HOLD OF HIM AND I WILL NOT
LET HIM GO UNTIL I BRING HIM INTO MY
MOTHER'S HOUSE, INTO THE CHAMBER OF
HER WHO CONCEIVED ME.*[1]   *Sg 3:4.*

Discussion of this verse still engages us: 'I
have taken hold of him and I will not let
him go'. Should such anxious care be
exercised that your Beloved, once caught,
be detained? If he is a Bridegroom he will return love
for love. Does he not cling to you of his own accord?
Is he not bound fast of his own volition? The impatient
jealousy of lovers makes them rudely intrude even
when rebuffed and bitter rivalry cures them of shy-
ness.*   But now you say: 'I will not let him go', as if   *Sg 8:6.*
he would seek to escape were he not tenaciously
restrained. If he loves, how will he want to escape or

consent to be torn away? Or are you moved perhaps
by a lover's suspicions and a superfluous fear of
losing him, thanks to your great desire to retain him?
Well, fear is not superfluous where the issue is doubtful. Amid perils, dread is not superfluous. But you
should dread rather your own fickleness. He is God
and is not changeable. The fickleness inborn in you is
close to a fall and through the unsteady emotion of a
distracted mind you are most easily swept away if
you do not cling fast.

2. Now let us apply these words to the early
Church. Indeed they seem to belong to her, as, with
the boldness of the prophets, she defended for herself the rights of faith and charity against the assaults
of persecution. Consider how many attempted to
dissolve or defile this spiritual marriage of Christ and
the Church. Contemplate also the beginnings of the
infant Church,[2] when like a new bride she was
hastening to Christ's first embraces. What fury, what
fraud, O good Jesus, did she endure in those days!

1 Co 11:19.
2 Tm 3:12.

Fitting indeed it was that heresies exist,* that there
be persecutions,* in order that she might cling to her
Beloved the more tenaciously, the more violently she
saw herself torn from faith in him or witness to him.
'Who shall separate us', said Paul on behalf of the

Rm 8:35.

whole Church, 'from the love of Christ?'* But in
those days the truth of faith was not corrupted
nor the freedom of witness strangled. 'For Sion's
sake', says Isaiah, 'I will not be silent and for the sake

Is 62:1.

of Jerusalem I will not be quiet'.* The disciples, after
being scourged in the Synagogue, were ordered to
keep silent. Yet for Sion's sake they do not keep
silent and for the sake of that carnal Jerusalem they

Ac 5:40-42.

do not rest.*

Truly the Synagogue is carnal, for she extinguished
the life-giving Spirit in herself and tries to snuff it out
in the Church. She did not see fit to acknowledge the

Rm 1:28. See
Bernard, SC 62:
3; SBOp 2:156,
13-15.

truth about Christ. Therefore she was abandoned to a
false interpretation.* She disapproved of the stone
once approved; she rejected the stone once

Ps 117:22.

elected.* She held fast to the law but knew not
Christ. She 'took away the key of knowledge' but

neither entered herself nor allowed others to enter.* *Lk 11:52.*
Why do you shut the door upon us to whom Christ
opened it? Upon his shoulder is 'the key of the house
of David' which he opens and no one closes, closes *Is 22:22; Rv 3:12.*
and no one opens.* He opened to the Gentiles and *Antiphon of Ves-*
closed to the Jews. For 'blindness has fallen on Israel *pers, 20 December*
in part', that 'the fullness of the Gentiles might
enter'.* Blind is Judaea and, behind the veil of the *Rm 11:25.*
letter, she knows not how to find the door.

The Synagogue proclaims the veil of the letter but
disclaims the truth, neither explaining nor distinguishing correctly. She would distinguish correctly, if she
distinguished the observance of the letter from its
meaning, if she allotted one time for the antiquity
of the letter and another for the freshness of its meaning. For there is a time to mend and a time to rend.* *Qo 3:7.*
Simultaneously was the letter proclaimed and the
meaning foretold. But in the letter is the image, and
beneath the images is the meaning. The Church now
distinguishes the meaning and rends what was sewn
together; but if on occasion the Synagogue knows the
literal meaning according to the flesh, she no longer
knows him whom, as it were, she cradled in swad-
dling clothes but rejected when his identity was
disclosed.

3. The Church says: 'I have taken hold of him and
I will not let him go'. The Synagogue rejects him, indeed insults him, but the Church does not shrink 'from
the voice of insult and reproach nor from the face of an
enemy or persecutor'.* In Matthew, the wicked servant *Ps 43:17.*
says in his heart: 'My lord delays in coming',* and *Mt 24:48.*
therefore he strikes the servants of his lord because they
already know and announce his coming; but 'for Sion's
sake' they do not keep silent and 'for the sake of Jerusalem' are not quiet.* Persecutors can scourge the *Is 62:1.*
body but they cannot drive Christ from the spirit.
Affection for Christ is entwined in hearts more
stoutly than the thongs of the lash. They were
scourged in the Synagogues, cast into prison, dragged
before the courts, but they rejoice in all this, because
'they have been found worthy to suffer insult for the
name of Jesus'.* *Ac 5:41.*

'I have taken hold of him and I will not let him go'. The bride took hold because she did not fear. She did not fear while all the earth quaked and the greater powers of this world were changed into a heart of bitterness against her.* She was bound to the Bridegroom with a rope which could not be broken, the rope of charity, a rope which cannot fail because charity never fails.* She acted confidently because she held fast in charity. For 'anyone who clings to God is one spirit with him'* and 'where the Spirit of the Lord is there is freedom'.* Therefore she acted freely and maintained the unwavering witness of her hope.* In the early days, faith seemed indeed to be sheer folly and witness a good reason for shame. Why do I say 'shame'? It was a matter of the utmost danger. Yet they were unable 'to fear those who kill the body',* for the spirit of life was before their face, Christ the Lord.* So they more readily allowed themselves to be torn from their flesh than from his charity. The bride reserved nothing of herself, that she might hold him fast. That is why she says: 'I have taken hold of him and I will not let him go'. She did indeed cling to him strenuously amid so many adversaries and persecutors, even while the age of faith was still in its infancy.

4. 'Until I bring him into my mother's house.' Our faith has at last been brought into safety. There is no one to attack it openly, but former persecutors have become adherents and former adversaries have become leaders. At last the faith has been brought from the hedges into the house, from the sea into harbor. The fury of persecuting princes has turned into favor and heretics with their wily caviling refuted by the clear truth of Catholic faith have fallen silent. At last our faith, and with it Christ, has been 'rescued from the opposition of the people'. At last he has been 'placed at the head of the nations',* no longer 'posted as a sign to be contradicted'.* After the blood and tears of so many martyrs in conflict for the faith of Christ, after the Church withstood the violence of so many persecutors and frustrated the wiles

Ps 45:3.

1 Co 13:8.

1 Co 6:17.
2 Co 3:17.

Heb 10:23.

Mt 10:28.
Lm 4:20.

Ps 17:44.
Lk 2:34.

of so many heretics, now that there is no longer a stumbling-block but a joy in the Cross of Christ,* and we have become not a spectacle for this world to deride but a triumph of grace,* after she weathered so many perils, does not the Church of Christ seem to you as it were, to have brought her Beloved from the field of battle and labor into the chamber of peace and repose?[3]

1 Co 1:23;
Ga 6:14.

1 Co 4:9;
Col 2:14-15.

5. You see then, in the beginnings of the new-born Church, the care needed lest her Beloved, so long desired and at last embraced, be torn from her. So what will happen from now on, now that the Beloved has been brought into safety by faith and, as it were, into the bridal chamber? Hereafter will there be room for sloth and shall we bid farewell to diligence? Shall he be imperilled in the calm, who could not be in the storm? Or is he not in peril, who is at death's door? 'Faith without works is dead.'* The apostle commends faith but the faith 'which works through love'.* Where there is the labor of love or the love of labor, there is the life of faith.

Jm 2:20.

Ga 5:6.

What if, while truth is present in one's belief and freedom in its witness, life is absent through the absence of love? Then the cord is not of three strands and it is easily broken.* Scripturally, that freedom is illusory which does not spring from the root of charity and such witness does not so much rely on its own freedom as depend upon another's tolerance. Such witness is precarious, not its own master. It waits upon the favor of princes; it does not proceed from the warmth of faith. By the warmth of charity faith is stirred to life. Clearly faith is slothful in a threatening crisis, if it does not assert its freedom of witness prompted by love. Otherwise witness dies on the lips of the dead, as if he did not exist.

Qo 4:12.

Without charity then, faith is dead and witness is vain. The apostle says that 'Christ dwells by faith in our hearts'.* Surely not by faith which is dead! If inside is truth and outside life, then Christ is divided, for he is truth and life.* You have not yet fully introduced your Beloved, when he is half outside. What if you failed to introduce your Beloved? For

Ep 3:17.

Jo 14:6.

how is he your Beloved, if charity is not joined to faith? 'Christ risen from the dead dies now no more',* but to himself he dies no more. Take care lest he die to you, or rather lest you die to him. Again, what love can exist in or be shown to the dead? On what grounds then will he be called Beloved, where no love exists? If Christ dwells in your heart by faith* but dwells outside for lack of love, I fear—or rather it is certain—that in you he is either half alive or wholly dead. 'I live', says Paul, 'no longer I, but Christ lives in me.'*

6. You can also make these words your own, provided you also can say with Paul: 'The charity of God has been poured into our hearts through the Holy Spirit who has been given to us'.* But in some this Christ-life is full of labor, in others full of freedom, but in a few spiritual persons it is alive with delights. Yet if until now you have wholly surrendered to the dominion of the flesh, if a ready and familiar access to the recesses of your heart lies open for the princes of darkness, and if you have prostituted your soul to unclean lovers, what covenant will you have with Christ about Belial, what fellowship with light about darkness?* If, however, for the love of Christ you have declared war on vice and the prompter of vice, then indeed you have taken hold of your Beloved but your ship is not yet at anchor. You are still buffeted and do not enjoy the calm of the bridal chamber. Your faith is in harbor, but you must still either disperse or flee before the gusts of bad habit and the clouds of emerging or frequent temptations.

Hold him fast in crises, lest your Beloved escape you before you 'bring him into your mother's house, into the chamber of her who conceived you'. Hold him fast with might and main, lest he elude you more quickly for [your] relaxing caution and care. Hold him fast by faith and by your vocation. Hold him fast by your behavior and by your way of life, and do not release him. The struggle from now on is not for the truth of the faith; the fires of the present spiritual battle rage unabated against good morals and an

Rm 6:9.

Ep 3:17.

Ga 2:20.

Rm 5:5.

2 Co 6:15.

upright life. Perilous times threaten us in these last days, when men are 'lovers of self, covetous, haughty'*, inventors and indeed abettors of evil. At the birth of the Christian faith a vast persecution of this name broke out. Today a plague of immorality, fetid enough and growing relentlessly, spreads its foul breath. Bad example surely corrupts good morals.* Attract us, good Jesus, with the fragrance of your ointments, lest an infectious blast rise in our vicinity to spoil the salt of wisdom within us. 'Let your speech always be gracious, seasoned with salt', says Paul.* Is it only speech and not rather sight, hearing, gait—in a word the whole of our outward deportment which must be seasoned with salt? 'Try to please all men in everything, just as I do', says Paul.* But if the princes of the Church lose their savor with what will the people be seasoned?[4]

2 Tm 3:1-2; Rm 1:30; 2 M 1:1.

1 Co 15:33.

Col 4:6.

1 Co 10:33.

7. We brothers, who make profession of religious life, ought also to be the salt of the earth. If then in us also 'the salt becomes tasteless, with what will it be salted'?* The priest also has become like the people, that the people with greater abandon may become like the priest. Monks assiduously conform themselves to the world and those in the world astutely enough and quite literally have a pretext for their error in our example. Shepherds and people, seculars and religious, by mutual example either instruct or encourage one another in vice. Their maws are stuffed with vice, belching from one to another the pestilential breath of a behavior that is either foul or lukewarm. Alas, how avidly the lips of our heart draw in this foul breath and breathe this corrupting air! This plague on all sides flows in through our windows.*

Mt 5:13.

Jr 9:21.

Good Jesus, when, if ever, will morals be as blameless as faith is incorrupt? When will it come about that as peace coexists with truth, so there may be no battle for virtue? When shall we embrace the whole of you, and by choice, in the chamber of contemplation and repose?[5] Few exist in the Church who have reached this state, yet for their part they declare: 'I have taken hold of him and I will not let him go until I bring him into my mother's house, into the chamber of her who conceived me.' Not the entire person of the Church, yet a large part is such that she can utter these words: 'I have taken hold of him and I will not let him go until I bring him into my mother's house, into the chamber of her who conceived me'. Faith is more abundant but works of charity are limited.

Is this distinction to be observed in the whole body of believers and not also in each one of us? For who will be found, whose fullness of devout affection consistently matches the fullness of his real and unquestioned faith? Great indeed is he—if there be such a one—who as he never falters in faith, so is not troubled by any passions in his spirit. Such a person, I would say, has indeed entered into the secrets of the chamber. A good chamber is tranquillity of heart. With some persons, wisdom is in labor, but with the humble and tranquil the Spirit of the Lord reposes and 'his place is in peace'.* But here let our sermon repose for a while, or rather may our understanding rest in this secret of the chamber, that what experience shall have taught may return more clearly in the next sermon, by the gift of our Lord Jesus Christ, who with the Father and the holy Spirit lives and reigns, God for ever and ever. Amen.

Ps 75:3.

NOTES TO SERMON THIRTEEN

1.   The sermon addresses one individual, as Miquel notes in *Citeaux* 27 (1965) 151, in a citation from par. 6; *et nos fratres,* of paragraph 7, is only an apparent exception, for the sentence refers to Gilbert and his reader.

2.   Reading *lactentis Ecclesiae* for *latentis Ecclesiae.*

3.   Leclercq, *Otia Monastica,* 106:20.

4.   Reading *salientur* rather than *salient.*

5.   Leclercq, *Otia Monastica,* 119:22.

SERMON 14,
THE VIGIL IN SLEEP

She sleeps but her heart leaps to her Beloved.
1. The bride should not be wakened from sleep
with her Beloved. 2. Gazelles and hinds mean
alacrity of mind and nimbleness of spirit.
3. Hinds mean longevity and gazelles keenness
of vision. 4. The restless disturb the quiet of
spiritual persons. 5. Contemplation elicits com-
passion, and transport of mind makes one
considerate of the weak. 6. The more freedom
the bride has for leisure and contemplation, the
more fruit she will bring back to her handmaids.
7. Daughters of Babylon are subjects who
trouble superiors by grumbling; 8. they arrogate
to themselves the judgement of God.

I ADJURE YOU, DAUGHTERS OF JERUSALEM,
BY THE GAZELLES AND THE HINDS OF THE
FIELDS, THAT YOU DO NOT AROUSE OR
AWAKEN THE BELOVED UNTIL SHE HERSELF
PLEASES*[1]   Sg 3:5.

Obviously, since such an adjuration is
made on her behalf, the bride has fallen
asleep. Why should she not sleep with
her Beloved on entering her mother's
chamber, the retreat of delights? She sleeps when she
experiences a transport of mind at the approach of
her Beloved. 'I adjure you', he says, 'not to arouse
the beloved'. Blessed obviously is she who is allowed
to hold her Beloved and is not obliged to release

him. Hold fast what you hold, hold and touch
lingeringly and lovingly the word of life. Unroll the
the scroll of life, the scroll which Jesus unrolls or,
rather, which is Jesus. Wrap yourself in him, wrap
yourself in that fine linen in which he was wrapped,
for he was clothed in light as in a garment.* Put on
your Beloved, our Lord Jesus Christ.† Carve out
lovingly for yourself a room in the rock, a new tomb
'in which no one has as yet been laid'.*

Christ is indeed the rock.* New things can always
be discovered in Christ. Into the new, one may penetrate. In him are many retreats, countless treasures of
wisdom.* He is not exhausted in one shearing of his
fleece; he can be shorn very often. Mystical senses,
sacred affections are good fleeces. In such Jesus
abounds; he cannot be left naked and despoiled.
'I shall rejoice', says the psalmist, 'over your words as
one who has found *much spoil*'.* Clothe yourself in
this spoil, wrap yourself in these fleeces, that your
sides, as it is written, may grow warm,* for his word
is a flame.* Herein repose,² that your sleep may be
sweet, as Solomon says.* In our text, the Bridegroom
also guards and cherishes this sleep of his beloved,
forbidding that she be awakened. 'I adjure you', he
says, 'by the gazelles and the hinds of the field.'
Clearly this is a novel adjuration, not more wonderful
in its verbal form than in the depth of its mystery.

2. When I enquire what mystery lies wrapped in
these animals. I understand that they typify some
alacrity of a free mind and the nimbleness of a spirit
which, so to speak, by leaps and bounds transports
itself to higher levels. Do some persons not seem to
you like gazelles and hinds³ who, though dwelling in
the body, nonetheless have leapt over the obstacles
of the body and in lightness of spirit feel almost no
weight of the flesh and, thanks to their minds, are
unaware of this mass of earthly clay? Walking in the
spirit they no longer feel the desires of the flesh,* or
if they feel these desires, feel them only languishing
and, as it were, gasping and drawing their last
breath. To such persons Paul says: 'You are not in the
flesh but in the spirit'.* Again he says: 'Even if we

Mk 15:46;
Ps 103:2.
†Rm 13:14.

Is 22:16; Mt 27:
60; Lk 23:53.

1 Co 10:4.

Col 2:3.

Ps 118:162.

Jb 31:20.

Pr 3:24.

Ga 5:16.

Rm 8:9.

have known Christ in the flesh, we no longer know
him so'.* Now he has become wholly spiritual, now   *2 Co 5:16.*
he has betaken himself to the solitudes of heaven,
now he has ascended to higher levels. Therefore the
Church says: 'My Beloved is like a gazelle and a fawn
of hinds . . . upon the hills of Bether'.*   *Sg 2:9, 17.*

To these hills Paul invites you when he says: 'If
you have risen with Christ, seek the things which are
above'.* Paul would have you resemble a spiritual   *Col 3:1.*
gazelle as he summons you to those heavenly hills,
for he clothes you as the image of that unique young
hind. 'As we have borne the likeness of the earthly
one, let us bear also the likeness of the one from
heaven.'* Paul himself is a good hind when he says: *1 Co 15:49.*
'Our homeland is in heaven';* obviously he is a good   *Ph 3:20.*
hind, fed and guided by the Spirit of the Lord, for the
Spirit of the Lord is nimble and agile.* Good are the *Ws 7:22.*
hinds whom the voice of the Lord trains, to whom he
reveals the lair of his mysteries,* the lair in which *Ps 28:9.*
that blessed young hind lies concealed. Good surely
is the gazelle, which can respond with mettlesome
and unflagging devotion of spirit to everything proposed or imposed: 'My heart is ready, O God, my
heart is ready'; forgetting what lies behind, it bounds
to what lies ahead.*   *Ps 56:8; Ph 3:13.*

3. You have heard the common traits of these
animals; now hear what is proper to each, that we
may draw some distinction between them and that
our treatment of each may not be confused and
indistinct. In hinds, notice their longevity and, in
gazelles, their keenness of vision. Hinds are said to
preserve themselves from old age by a natural ability
and by a vivifying renewal to summon from dissolu-
tion a life in decline. Christ in a special way is
described not as a hind but as a young hind; he relies
on eternal youth and has no ingredient of age which
might later require renewal. In a unique way he is a
gazelle in his privileged vision. According to Matthew,
no one knows the Father but the Son and one to
whom he chooses to reveal him.* Everything is naked   *Mt 11:27.*
and open to his eyes. Consequently they also are
likened to spiritual gazelles who have the eyes of

Ep 1:17.

their mind unveiled by recognizing God;* who, once having become spiritual, distinguish and discern all things; who with faces uncovered contemplate the glory of the Lord.* However, they are hinds because they are transformed into the same image from splendor to splendor, as if by the Spirit of the Lord;* because they slough off the old man and don the new who 'was created in the justice and holiness of truth';* because they again restore to new fervor a devotion beginning to dodder and languish from tedium and because they know nothing of the ennui of perseverance, thanks to frequent renewal.

2 Co 3:18.

2 Co 3:18.

Ep 4:22-24.

'They who trust in the Lord', says Isaiah, 'will renew their strength', not to lose the old but to add new strength. They will renew their strength by frequently repeated additions. 'They will renew their strength', he says, 'they will run and not grow weary, they will walk and not grow faint'.* This renewal resembles a constant resumption of marches forward without retreat or weariness. Good indeed is the strength which, though it runs with an effort, knows not how to turn back in defeat. Better, of course, is the strength which without noticing the discomfort of effort leaps over the stumbling-blocks of an ambush and races on flying hoofs over the open plain, as Jeremiah says[4] 'the nimble courser bolts across its desert paths'.*

Is 40:31.

Jr 2:23.

4. That is why our text speaks of hinds of the fields, because anything rugged or steep is for them level and open and accessible to their unimpeded flight, like the ranges of an open plain. The voice of the Lord is the voice of intimate inspiration flowing gently into the ears of the mind. That is surely the voice which trains hinds such as these and discloses his lairs to them. For if there are any hiding places overgrown with a thick tangle of scandals as if with brambles, they are not impenetrable for those whose feet the Lord makes like the hoofs of hinds, who cannot be hindered by any harmful obstacle but rather take pleasure in hardship and are trained to accept wrongs or to take them in stride in their passionate desire to hasten to the heights and

to forge ahead.

Oh, in what pitiful times we live! How is it that nearly all of us bound away from this rule to its opposite and construe as wrongs even things which give every appearance of piety? Almost everywhere we suffer setbacks, we stumble on level ground and our footsteps have been made slippery in the streets, as Jeremiah says.* We complain that everything is a hindrance for us, because 'the path of the laggard is like a hedge of thorns'.* We rejoice over opportunities for complaint, we are so full of suspicion that, as it is written,[5] 'the rustle of a falling leaf' seems to terrify us,* and by word and deed we try to court trouble for our spirit. Hence too often we disturb the quiet of spiritual men, interrupt their leisure, disturb the sleep of a mind bent on higher things and wrest it from the most welcome embrace of the Bridegroom.[6]

Lm 4:18.

Pr 15:19.

Lv 26:36.

5. Annoyances of this sort therefore, either sought by perversity or brought on by weakness, the Bridegroom diverts from his beloved; he invites the daughters of Jerusalem to some spiritual alacrity. For this is the purpose of his adjuring them by gazelles and hinds: to spur them to emulate spiritual men and to refrain from insistently pestering his beloved: 'I adjure you not to arouse the beloved until she herself pleases'. It is useful for you that the beloved awaken, but wait until it suits her. Let her choice be awaited, for care of you pertains to her office. She will choose, when the Spirit teaches her to choose. The anointing of the Spirit will instruct her, for by clinging to her Beloved she has become one spirit with him.* Therefore she can say: 'The Spirit of the Lord is upon me, because he has anointed me', sent me to proclaim good tidings.* Therefore she will bring you the good tidings, when from the Spirit she has learned the hour. Meanwhile in her thirst let her drink in what she may pour out more copiously.

1 Jo 2:27;
1 Co 6:17.

Is 61:1.

The grace of contemplation does not exclude, but elicits, compassion, and transport of mind makes one considerate of the weak. For while Adam sleeps, the man's rib gently softens into the weaker sex and, for the sake of companionship, from the side of a man was formed a woman, or rather Adam himself is changed into a woman companion and by a kind of conformation becomes his own wife. Therefore when he awakens he utters his first word, a word of charity as he recognizes himself in his consort: 'this at last is bone of my bones and flesh of my flesh!'* Does not Paul seem to you to transform his manly dignity into the lowlier sex, when he says that he has been made infirm for the infirm?* Like a spiritual Adam he becomes Eve, while the apostle's firmness compassionates his subjects and the loftiness of his virtue and knowledge bends down to the capacity of the infirm, exchanging his wine for their milk. Indeed, if he is carried out of his mind for God, he becomes sober for others.* Transport of mind is a good sleep; far from arousing pride, it teaches sobriety.

'I adjure you not to arouse the beloved until she herself pleases', and if in the meantime she is 'carried out of her mind for God', still she will become sober again. If now she sleeps, she will awaken again and pour out for you in due measure the wine she discovers. She knows when to 'provide rations for her household and food for her handmaids'.* How will she not pity the daughters of her womb,* when she does not overlook her handmaids? Yet good daughters count themselves handmaids and ignore their native liberty while they recall that they were set free by the spirit of truth. For they are truly free who are set free by truth, and therefore they ignore any other liberty, because they rejoice that they were liberated by adoption. According to Scripture, the more gratuitous is adoption, the more devout is self-effacement. The same persons then are handmaids and daughters, for where there is greater honour in adoption, there devotedness in submission is more justified.

6. 'Do not arouse her until she herself pleases.' She knows when to 'provide rations for her household and food for her handmaids'.* One need not fear her likeness to the daughter of Lamentations: 'The daughter of my people has grown cruel, like an

Marginal references:

Gn 2:23.
See S 20:8.

1 Co 9:22.

2 Co 5:13.

Pr 31:15.
Is 49:15.

Pr 31:15.

ostrich in the desert'.* An ostrich has the semblance
of wings but in fact is unable to fly. It knows not how
to fly by a transport of mind;[7] therefore it does not
visit its own image but 'abandons its eggs on the
ground . . . . It forgets that a foot may trample them
or a wild beast crush them'.* An ostrich does not
know how to soar to the slumber of contemplation
and therefore does not clothe itself in feelings of
compassion. But the falling asleep of a mother in
transport of mind is in the interest of her daughters
and it is wholly for their gain that her spiritual slumber is prolonged. That is why the Bridegroom says:
'I adjure you not to arouse the beloved until she herself pleases'. Good is the adjuration by which the
mother is spared and the progress of her daughters is
sought. For the more freedom she has for leisure and
contemplation, the more fruit she will bring back to
her handmaids. The more lofty the heights of her
ascent, the more lowly her descent and the more
fruitful her condescension.

Why do you want to ration the times which the
Bridegroom has reserved to the will of the beloved?
'Do not arouse her', he says, 'until she herself
pleases'. She will be pleased, when the vision of her
Beloved has fled from her eyes. His presence is fleeting and vanishes suddenly. 'I belong to my Beloved',
she says, 'and his desire is for me.'* Why try to interrupt so holy an exchange before the alloted time?*
Blessed is this converse but brief is its hour. Brief
enough is the hour; why desire to shorten it further?
Nothing should be subtracted from so brief a
moment. Meantime let her freely enjoy the fleeting
hour. Do you wish to arouse and claim for yourselves her, whom Christ arouses and keeps awake in
himself? As the Canticle says, although she is asleep,
her heart keeps vigil in Christ.* Peter and his companions on the mountain were overcome with sleep
and waking saw the Majesty of Jesus. They were
happily overcome with sleep, since in them human
perception was suspended. What depended upon
themselves was overpowered and suspended in them,
that becoming blind and insensitive to the things of

Lm 4:3.

Jb 39:14-15.

Sg 7:10.
Lam, p. 188,
n. 117.

Sg 5:2.

the world but aroused by the divine spirit, they might be awake to recognize only the things of God.

Lk 9:32. 'Awaking', says Luke, 'they saw his Majesty'.*

Happily then does he keep vigil, who sees such visions, who sees the glory of the Only-begotten of the Father, who hears hidden words which man has no license to speak. Mysteries may not be spoken to one in whom the Son of God has not yet risen. 'See that you tell no one about the vision', says Matthew, *Mt 17:9.* 'until the Son of Man rises from the dead'.* The vision cannot be spoken to one in whom Christ has not yet risen. Again something similar was said to Mary: 'Do not touch me, for I have not yet ascended *Jn 20:17.* to the Father'.* It may not be spoken to one who is not caught up into paradise, into the place of delights, into the place of which Peter said: 'It is good *Mt 17:4.*
2 Co 12:4. for us to be here'.* Happily is one aroused, who with Paul is caught up into this paradise,* who with Peter ascends the mountain, who can watch with Christ if *Mt 26:40.* only for one hour,* whom no mortal touches, that Christ may arouse him and make him keep vigil. Peter also he touched and therefore Peter kept vigil and saw his Majesty. In our text, see the change in the beloved as she rises from the embrace of the Bridegroom: 'Who is she', we read, 'who ascends . . . like a *Sg 3:6.* column of smoke?'*

7. But for our part at this juncture let us now recall our soaring sermon and keep this verse for another beginning or rather for him who says of himself: 'I am the beginning, I who am speaking to *Jn 8:25.* you'.* For us may he be both the beginning of our sermon and the word of our heart, so that what we intend to speak about him, he may first speak within *See T 1:1.* us.* Speak, Lord, speak to me and speak for me. Reproach for me the daughters not of Jerusalem but of Babylon; tell the daughter of the Chaldaeans to be *Is 47:5.* seated and be silent.* God of goodness, how numerous today are the daughters of Babylon, who know not the canticles of Sion and thanks to whom 'we *Ps 136:2.* have hung up our harps'!* How numerous are the sons of Edom who drain and exhaust our spiritual gladness![8]

You restrain the daughters of Jerusalem from pestering the bride. O that you would spare me, O Lord, from the daughters of Babylon. For the annoyance of the malicious is different and much more distressing than that of lovers. Yet through some wretchedness of our times, even lovers have become malicious. 'What havoc' a friend 'wreaks in the sanctuary today'!* I should have said an enemy *Ps 73:3.* but I have expressed what causes greater grief. Our very friends have become enemies, friends by profession but enemies by disaffection, friends in appearance who disown the virtue of friendship. Absalom was a friend because he was a son; but 'what havoc' that criminal 'wrought in the sanctuary', that son upon his father, Absalom upon David! Absalom means 'his father's peace'. A good name, indeed, but he betrayed the excellence of his name. He coveted the kingdom; he defiled the bedchamber. Yet happy was David, for among so many sons only one rose to persecute him.

Among our teachers today, please name me one against whom only one Absalom sets a trap. Are not those men like so many Absaloms who, as Micah says, 'cry "peace" as long as they have food for their teeth'?* They covet their father's place, they defile *Mi 3:5.* his bedroom, while they corrupt their fellows with wicked whisperings; they pervert the hearts of the innocent, in which their father's spirit found pleasant repose. That man is an Absalom by imitation who usurps the place of his master and calumniates his life; he cries 'peace' and gnaws with his teeth. A poisonous gnawing is backbiting, a poisonous food of which Job says: 'Evil is sweet in his mouth and he hides it beneath his tongue'.* He hides it until in *Jb 20:12.* due course he may vomit forth the poison accumulated.

'What havoc' a friend 'wreaks in the sanctuary!' What his eye does not see his suspicion invents. 'They have set up their own signs as emblems and they have not understood'.* They set up what they *Ps 73:4-5.* do not discover; they set up what they later explain in a perverted sense. 'Their own signs', says the

Psalm, for they set themselves up as signs, when they
measure others by the rule of their own perversion.
'Signs', says the Psalm, as if to say: only emblems but
not reality, signs not of certainty but of suspicion.
'And they have not understood', for they rely not on
knowledge but on conjecture. 'The enemy wreaks
havoc in the sanctuary'.* In what sanctuary? In the
Holy of Holies, in that Holy One who says: 'He who
rejects you, rejects me'.* It is rash, as Paul says, to
judge another's servant.* Who, then, are you to
judge your own Lord? For he who questions
authority, questions the ordinance of God.*

8. Again God complains: 'Men have robbed me
of my judgement'.* 'Sons of men . . . why do you
love vanity and seek falsehood?'* You do indeed
covet the vanity of preferment and therefore in your
prelates you look for the falsehood of your evil
suspicions. For 'the sons of men are vain . . . false in
the scales',* false in their judgements. And would
that it were of but slight import for me to be judged
by men's light, while I await the judgement of the
eternal Day!* 'When I seize the appointed time', says
the psalmist, 'I will dispense strict justice'.* The just
Judge himself says that he awaits the time to dispense strict justice, and do you arrogate to yourself
the verdict before the time?* The Father has 'en-
trusted all judgement to the Son',* and do you arrogate to yourself a judgement which you have not
received, and that against your father? Beware lest
perhaps your judgement be against that Father from
whom 'all fatherhood in heaven and on earth takes
its name'.*

A race of vipers devours its mother and with
poisoned tooth gnaws at the life of its teacher.[9]
These are not daughters of Jerusalem, daughters of
peace, but the daughters of Babylon. When will you
rebuke them and tell them: 'Daughters' of Babylon,
'do not weep over me but over yourselves'?* For the
taunts against those who stand in your place redound
upon you and their grumbling is not against us but
against the Lord. Spare your grumbling then, which
does you no good and harms others.* Do you, O

Ps 73:3.

Lk 10:16.
Rm 14:4.

Rm 13:2.

Ezk 5:6.
Ps 4:3.

Ps 61:10.

1 Co 4:3-5.
Ps 74:3.

1 Co 4:5.
Jo 5:22.

Ep 3:15.

Lk 23:28.

*Ws 1:11. See
Miquel, p. 16,
n. 63.*

Lord, rather stop 'the mouths of those who speak
evil' and 'do not silence those who sing your
praises'.* But why do I linger any longer now over
these complaints? It is not my purpose at present to
weep for our woes but to sing the praise of others.
Let it suffice to have lamented our plight in brief. At
last I return from lamentations to lauds, deriving
spirit, eloquence and leisure from him who keeps
the restless away from the sleep of his Bride, Christ
Jesus who reigns with the Father and the Holy
Spirit for ever and ever. Amen.

Ps 62:12;
Est 13:17.

NOTES TO SERMON FOURTEEN

1.   This sermon addresses one individual throughout.

2.   See Leclercq, *Otia Monastica,* 117:15.

3.   For *caprea* and *cervus,* see Morson, pp. 161-2, 164, and White, pp. 42, 37-40.

4.   G. ignores the context which refers to a she-camel, and to a wild ass (v. 24). See White, pp. 79-83, Lam pp. 198-9, nn. 184, 191.

5.   See Horace, *Carmina,* 1:23, on the trembling fawn, *hinnuleus.*

6.   Cited by Leclercq, *Otia Monastica,* 97:73.

7.   See G. Ep 3:2, Morson, pp. 158-9, White, 121-2. G. does not 'directly contradict Jb 39:18', (Morson). The speed of the ostrich, attributable in part to its wings, allows it to outrun the horse and its rider, but need not mean that the ostrich soars.

8.   'The Edomites are charged with excessive glee at the fall of Jerusalem in 587, with counter-imprecations by Ps 137:7; Ob 10-12 (cf. 2 K 25:8-12)', *Jerome Biblical Commentary,* p. 217, article by Ignatius Hunt OSB.

9.   Mt 3:7, Ws 16:10; see Morson, p. 160; White, p. 170; Aeschylus, *Choephori,* lines 540-50.

SERMON 15,
ENAMORED, HUMBLED AND RENEWED

Close to Christ, the bride is enamored,
humbled, renewed in all virtues. 1. She is
renewed in Christ by prayer and meditation,
as gold in the forge. 2. She knows that the
world is a desert but that Christ is a fertile
field. 3. A good desert is the heart barren of
vices, the soul and the body without the weeds
of vices; a good desert is the womb of vir-
ginity watered with streams from Lebanon,
bearing the fruit of Christ, who is called the
wind for he dries up the waters of vice and
sends apostles and saints on their way. 4. Pass-
ing fervor is compared to a column of smoke.
5. May our vices be consumed and our virtues
rarified in the fire of Christ. 6. Myrrh, incense,
and perfumer's powder are explained, and
three types of prayer distinguished. 7. Per-
fumer's powder is a symbol of humility;
humility of vanity is distinguished from humil-
ity of reality. 8. Suffering and contradiction
are a stimulus to humility. 9. The dust of
humility yields to the fire of charity.

WHO IS SHE WHO ASCENDS THROUGH THE
DESERT LIKE A COLUMN OF SMOKE FROM
SPICES OF MYRRH AND INCENSE AND ALL
THE POWDERS OF THE PERFUMER?*[1]   *Sg 3:6.*

'**W**ho is she who ascends through the desert like a column of smoke from spices?' See, brothers, as indeed you do see, how effective for the increase of grace is tranquillity of mind. See what kind of fruit Christ's beloved reaps from interior repose.[2] See her appearance, I say, as she emerges from the embrace of her Bridegroom. But do not ask me about her appearance as she emerges; consult rather the companions of the Bridegroom. What if even in their eyes she emerges from the hidden embrace of her Beloved in a new and unfamiliar appearance? It is obviously new, for the novelty arouses their wonder: 'Who is she who ascends?' Notice her progress. In previous verses she accosts the watchman and asks about their vision of her Beloved. Here she emerges, a marvel to the watchmen and with a new look. Why should she not emerge renewed from the breast of her Beloved? For it is he who says of himself:

Rv 21:5.

'Behold, I make all things new'.*

Even new things he renews. Picture him as a forge; surrender your gold. If the gold is pure, he returns it more refined and the red hot metal reflects a brightness still fresh from the forge. Is Christ not a forge?

Ps 118:140.

'Your word', says the psalmist, 'is a raging fire'.* What has become molten in this forge can emerge only as a new and a different creature in Christ. While he prayed, as Luke says, his own appearance

Lk 9:29.

changed;* but even while you pray, for your sake his own appearance is changed! For remaining one in himself, he renews all other things. The bodily appearance of the Lord was changed as he prayed and thereby he wished to bring home to your mind the power of prayer, because prayer makes you different in your inmost being and meditation changes you into a new self and renews you. 'With our unveiled faces reflecting like mirrors the brightness of the Lord', says Paul, 'we are turned into the image

2 Co 3:18.

which we reflect',* that is, we are transformed into the very image we gaze upon.

2. Perhaps the bride also emerged from the sanctuary of contemplation robed in the image of

the Bridegroom upon which she was gazing. She is
obviously new. For the wonder of his companions
over her witnesses to her newness. 'Who is she who
ascends?'—as if one should say: she has changed
since yesterday and the day before. She no longer
makes her rounds of the city, she does not scurry
through the streets and squares and past the watchmen. She does not stray aimlessly but ascends in a
direct route. What is this renewal so sudden within
herself? 'Who is she who ascends', and ascends
'through the desert?' Deserted, indeed, arid and
barren does she consider all this world through which
she ascends. And for what reason has the scent of
this desert become for us 'like the scent of a fertile
field' as if 'the Lord has blessed it'?* How many   *Gn 27:27.*
does the scent of this desert lure to itself and hold
without possibility of escape? This scent is 'the
scent of death luring to death'.* What you consider   *2 Co 2:16.*
fruitfulness is emptiness! 'It is a land of thirst', says
Jeremiah, and 'the image of death'.* 'A land of   *Jr 2:6.*
thirst', for it provokes rather than satisfies worldly
lusts. Fruitless is the land you think bountiful and, if
there is any fruit, it withers so fast that by its own
disappearance it presents a picture of death. Where
you behold the picture of death, why suppose you
are smelling the fragrance of life? Bountifulness
really breathes forth the fragrance of Christ. He is
indeed the field really full and fertile, the field
which the Father has blessed. The bride knows no
other field than his; any other she considers a desert,
an alkaline wasteland.

3. 'Who is she who ascends through the desert?'
Your heart will surely be a good desert, if it has not
been furrowed by an enemy's plough, if it has not
been watered by his rain or dyed with his dew, if the
cockle he sows does not grow rank in you or rather
spring up afresh as in fertile soil. Let your heart be
barren, lest it produce such a weed or receive such a
seed. 'My soul', says the psalmist, 'is like land without water in your sight'.* A good desert is such a   *Ps 142:6.*
soul, but a good desert also is flesh entire, flesh
not harrowed by unclean desires, flesh ignorant of

the seeds of carnal pleasure. 'For he who sows in the

Ga 6:8.

flesh, will reap corruption from the flesh.'* In Scripture, a good desert is a virginal womb. Such was the womb of that blessed and unique virginity which no wound of immodest emotion or impure affection violated. Her flesh was like wasteland, pathless and unwatered, wherein Christ appeared. Yet her flesh was not wholly barren, since it gave birth to Christ; it is watered, but with streams of virtues. Therefore her flesh is called 'a well of living waters, flowing in

Sg 4:15.

a torrent from Lebanon',* because the limpid stream of virginal purity pours forth spiritual graces. 'A garden enclosed' was her womb, through the discipline of virginal chastity, because the heat of carnal desire did not destroy the hedge of innocence. Therefore, watered by such streams, her womb

Ps 1:3.

yielded fruit in due season.*

Do you wish to hear what kind of fruit this wasteland yielded? Hosea teaches you for he says: 'The Lord will bring a scorching wind ascending from the

Ho 13:15.

desert and will dry up the springs' of death.* Who else dried up the springs of death but Christ Jesus, whom the desert of an inviolate womb poured forth for us? Rightly did Hosea say 'wind', because the

Lm 4:20.

Spirit before our face is Christ the Lord.* Again he was called the second 'Adam who came as a life-giving

1 Co 15:45.
Is 60:8.

spirit'.* At his breath fly the clouds of apostles which surprised Isaiah.* Why be surprised that he is

Is 19:1.

called a wind, when Isaiah also calls him a cloud? 'The Lord shall ascend upon a cloud.'* Here do not understand 'light' as 'scudding' and 'unstable', but take 'lightness' to mean 'spiritual readiness', because an incorruptible body laid no burden on the soul and an earthly dwelling did not oppress a mind which

Ws 9:15; Lk 2:19.

stores many, or rather all, thoughts.*

Are not all the saints like winds because, eluding things of earth by lightness of spirit, they build for

Ph 3:20.

themselves a homeland in heaven?* But He himself is a wind for a special reason, for 'he walks above the wings of all other winds' and surpasses the virtues

Ps 103:3; Ep 1:21;
1 P 3:22.

of all the spirits.* Rightly therefore does Hosea call him a wind and a scorching wind, because at his

breath the frosts of sin in us were thawed and our
captivity melted like a flash flood in the south.* In
the warmth of this wind the disciples felt themselves
enflamed when they asked: 'Were not our hearts
burning within us while he was speaking?'* And I
know not whether he blows anywhere more freely
than in the untrodden desert of a chaste and inviolate integrity. Through these he blows freely, and
the soul in a chaste body he makes glow with the
fervor of charity. That soul, melted with spiritual
desires, he dissolves into light vapor and makes rise
like a column of smoke.

Ps 125:4.

Lk 24:32.

4. 'Who is she who ascends through the desert
like a column of smoke?' A good desert is the flesh
drained and dried by the virtue of chastity, for it
exhales no mist of impure pleasure, does not ex-
tinguish but rather feeds the fire which the breath of
the Lord enkindles. If this fire finds a soul full of
spices, it sets the soul alight, changes it into another
shape and wafts it into the upper air like a column of
smoke. 'Like a column', because by the disciplining
of its thoughts the soul has been restored from dissipation to recollection and directed from lower to
higher levels.[3] 'Like a column', because the soul both
gathers itself together and reaches beyond itself.

But what is meant by the comparison of the soul
to a column of 'smoke'? Did the text wish perhaps to
hint by this comparison that the grace of this spiritual
sweetness and ascent of the mind is not permanent
and solid but easily dissolves like smoke? The plumes
of smoke into which burnt incense dissolves are
obviously sweet-scented and wholly spiritual. But for
my part I fear for the coils of this soft and slender
column, lest gusts of wind buffet the column, lest
storms of anxiety sway it, lest breezes of temptation
scatter it, lest it yield to every wind. There are prece-
dents to awaken our apprehension. Indeed we see and
grieve for many pillars who fell as unexpectedly as
they rose suddenly. They are skilful in meditation,
keen on the study of prayer, rich in grace, fruitful in
tender devotion, profuse in tears; then suddenly some
slight occasion for impatience makes their spiritual

delights sour and dry. When such a glorious ascent
so easily vanishes, is it not like smoke? Such an
ascent really is like a column of smoke when it either
crumbles through its own instability or yields to some
passing assault. Yet I dare not interpret the smoke as
a failing in the person of the bride. Still, if you dis-
agree for the sake of argument, you are welcome to
interpret her failure as the one described by the
psalmist: 'My eyes have failed with watching for
your promise. My soul has failed as it waits for your
salvation'.*

Ps 118:82-81.

5. Would that my eyes, O Lord, might grow dim
and fail me with this failure. Would that my soul
might fail with this failure. Would that it might fail
and dissolve and, melting at your word, that word
of passionate fire, be released from every plodding
act of understanding into the more rarified atmo-
sphere of a spiritual state. If there has been in me
any obtuseness of understanding[4] and dullness of
desire, may it dissolve into a habit of grace more
refined, and by some spiritual rarefaction and subtlety
be changed from its coarseness into a column of
smoke. Into such smoke may the power of my soul
vanish, but may it not vanish like smoke lest it
should say: 'My days have vanished like smoke'.*
For it is one thing to vanish like smoke so that you
vanish into non-existence, and quite another to
vanish so that you become like smoke, refined in
spirit and spiritual. The psalmist had become faint in
the right way when he said: 'My soul yearns and
faints for the courts of the Lord',* for how does he
not grow faint whom Christ inflames?

Ps 101:4.

Ps 83:3.

Christ is a fire, as Paul writes, and a 'consuming
fire'.* One who approaches me, He says, approaches
fire. Who will enable me to bind this fire to my
bosom,* that his fire may inflame my heart, change
my marrow and reduce me to nothing? Rightly the
bride ascends like a column of smoke, for she
emerges from the warmth of his chamber, from the
embrace of the flaming Word. Your flame, O Christ,
is wont to pour out clouds of incense; your flame
emits a smoke of aromatic fragrance. 'Like a column

Heb 12:29.

Pr 6:27.

of smoke from perfumes', says our text. In Job*
I read of smoke which billows from the jaws of
Leviathan,[5] and in the Apocalypse of smoke issuing
from the shaft of the bottomless pit,* but I read
nothing there either of a column or of spices. Nothing
upright is there, nothing fragrant is there, but only
utmost horror and total disorder. The smoke of error
issues from the shaft of the bottomless pit. Of this
smoke the wicked are said to admit: 'The breath in
our nostrils is a puff of smoke and words are sparks
to move our hearts'.[6]

Jb 41:11.

Rv 9:2.

May smoke, roused by your fire, good Jesus, be a
breath in my nostrils. May words from your forge be
sparks to move or rather to change my heart. Your
fire is a 'consuming fire'. Whatever vices it finds, it
consumes and it emits the smoke of confession. But
this smoke is not from spices. 'He touches the
mountains', says the psalmist, 'and they smoke'.*
Good is the fire which shrinks tumors of the spirit
and by its touch makes earthly exaltation vanish in
repentence like puffs of smoke. But of a different
fragrance and grace is the smoke which billows from
the burnt spices of the virtues. Your fire, the fire
which the Lord cast upon the earth and ardently
desired to see kindled,* not only consumes vices but
changes the virtues themselves into an affection of
more fragrant grace. When spices are whole they are
sweet-smelling, but when they are melted in this fire
they breathe out a much superior fragrance.

Ps 103:32.

Lk 12:49.

6. Perceiving this fragrance from the bride, the
Bridegroom's companions marvel and ask: 'Who is
she who ascends through the desert like a column of
smoke from spices of myrrh and incense and all the
powders of the perfumer?' In myrrh, you have the
virtue of continence; in incense, devotion to prayer;
in the powders of the perfumer, amid a wealth of
virtues, the humility of a contrite heart. Good is the
myrrh which subdues the petulance of the flesh,
allows no play to wanton impulses and strives to
compel the flesh not to be fleshy.* But the myrrh of
our continence seems corporeal, less chastened, like
a neighbor of the flesh, unless it has been melted in

Lam 188, n. 122.

this heavenly fire, this ardor of divine love. Good indeed is the myrrh of continence, when it checks an instinct hurrying towards what is illicit, but it is of a higher fragrance and grace when, melting in the heat of charity, it knows nothing of gross and carnal affection.

But what is the meaning of incense? Is its fragrance not slight as long as it is left uncrushed and solid? But when it begins to dissolve over the flames, it billows out wholly in coils of fragrant smoke. In a similar way, does not prayer seem to you gross and sluggish, delayed by the sloth of the body, if it has not been enkindled by the power of a blazing interior word? Certainly for my part, in incense I recognize the tinder of prayer and in smoke its grace. 'Let my prayer', says the psalmist, 'arise like incense in your sight'.* Prayer which has not been enkindled knows not how to go straight up to God. Prayer wrung from a cold heart falls back at once. If it is not eager, it cannot be lasting, for it suffers violence and is not its own master. Not that prayer enkindled is obviously its own master. The former is driven back despite its efforts; the latter is swept away beyond its efforts. The former strives and relapses; the latter ascends regardless of striving. The one is kept to its course by violence; the other is freely swept forward. One scarcely makes an appearance; the other cannot be restrained. One is born of labor; the other born of liberty. One is glum; the other joyous. One is good, but the other best. In Scripture, there is a prayer which in its moderation stands halfway between frigid and fervent, surpassing the former but not approaching the latter. And to put names on them, the first is forced, the second directed and the third ecstatic. The first I might call thirsty, the second sober, the third inebriated. Now the last is the prayer which goes out of its own mind to meet God,* and therefore 'ascends like a column of smoke from spices of myrrh and incense and all the powders of the perfumer'.

7. In the powders of the perfumer, the text marvelously represents the virtue of humility, for

Ps 140:2; Lam p. 191, nn. 137, 139, 142-43.

2 Co 5:13.

humility has not learned to make much of great
merits or to have much taste for lofty ideas,* but in
its humble opinion it makes little of the merits of its
other virtues and reduces their solid value, as it were,
to the consistency of powder. After the commenda-
tion of prayer, the text rightly adds a note about
humility under the figure of perfumer's powder. For
the prayer of one who humbles himself penetrates
the clouds.* Indeed, however keen prayer may be, it
is dull without the grace of humility. The myrrh of a
proud chastity emits an acrid scent and the myrrh of
continence which allows the spirit to grow wanton
with the smoke of pride does not properly restrain
the vagrant movements of carnal thoughts. By much
crushing, perfumes are reduced to powder. And
crushing is good, for God does not despise the
crushed and humbled heart.*

Obviously good is the crushing which leaves
nothing untouched, nothing elated, nothing not
humbled, even among the virtues. Humility sits in
judgement on acts of justice and convinces them not
only 'about sin but also about righteousness and
judgement'.* Now is what is convicted not, as it
were, crushed? Or is an act of justice which is put on
trial not humbled? 'In your truth', says the psalmist,
'you have humbled me'.* Not everyone can say this.
The weaker are humbled in their own vanity; the
more perfect are humbled in the truth of God. For
vanity cannot discern the truth, but truth can discern
both vanity and truth.

Yes, the Spirit discerns all things.* What seemed
whole and entire to human judgement, at his coming,
the Spirit of truth makes empty and crushed. For in
the mighty mortar of the Spirit perfumes of the virtues are to be ground into powder and justice to be
judged. 'In the whirlwind,' says Job, 'he will crush
me'; in the whirlwind of his spirit, a violent Spirit
that sweeps away my spirit in the whirlwind. 'In this
whirlwind,' says Job, 'he will crush me and multiply
my wounds'.* Before his violent Spirit arrived, my
justice seemed to me faultless; but the Spirit discerns,
crushes, wounds, and in many ways shatters my

Rm 11:20.

*Si 35:21; Lam
p. 188, n. 118,*

*Ps 50:19; Lam
p. 193, n. 155.*

Jo 16:8.

Ps 118:75.

1 Co 2:10.

Jb 9:17.

reliance on my good works. The Spirit teaches that
human virtue is wounded and faint.[7]

8.   Would that it might befall me to be crushed in
this way, to be reduced to the powder of all good

Lam 1:5-6, n. 103.   affections and devout meditations.* Good Jesus,
would that the whirlwind of your Spirit might
blow such a powder upon my soul, dust from the
squares of the heavenly Jerusalem, that in this dust
I might grow warm, in the dust I might be seated, in
the dust I might sleep—but in the dust of the perfumer's powder. Blessed is he who tarries in this
dust, he to whom fragrant thoughts pulverized by the
spirit are wafted from all sides. 'Awake', says

Is 26:19.   Isaiah, 'and give praise, you who dwell in the dust'.*
The bride also, waking from her happy sleep, rises
'like a column of smoke from spices . . . of·all the
powders of the perfumer'. 'All', says the text. Truth
in person teaches you to reduce the array of your
good works to a kind of powder and barrenness:
'When you have done all things, say "We are
unprofitable servants; we have done only what was

Lk 17:10.   our duty" '.*

Happy the man who gathers for himself powder of
such quantity and quality that he does whatever is
commanded and considers it nothing, who by humility crushes all the good things he gathers. Writing to
the Corinthians, Paul enumerates the many spices of
his good works: 'On frequent journeys, in perils from
floods, perils from brigands, perils from my own
nation, perils from the Gentiles, perils by sea, perils
in the city, perils in the wilderness, perils from false
brethren'. Then what does he add? 'The daily pres-
sure upon' him of his 'anxiety for all the Churches.
Who is weak', he asks, 'and I am not weaker? Who is

2 Co 11:26-29.   made to stumble and I am not indignant'?* Does
Paul not seem to you to have gathered a powder as it
were of good works, as he reviews these trials and
more like them? Would you care to hear of some
kinds of virtues in him still more sublime? Come with
him to the visions and revelations of God, to his
being swept into paradise, into the third heaven.
Come to that blessed ignorance of whether his

ecstasy took place in the body or out of the body. This was no longer the powder of humility but the incense of prayer. However, lest with this smoke of spiritual contemplation the smoke of vainglory be mingled, hear what follows: 'To keep me from being too elated by the greatness of these revelations, a sting was given me in the flesh'.* Paul is stung lest he be elated, and how is it that you who are listening to this shrink from being stung? How is it that amid a wealth of gifts you either cease to crush yourself or do not allow yourself to be crushed? A sting is a nuisance but the annoyance adds humility to your progress. A nuisance is a sting of the flesh but not a sting of charity. Suffering is bitter and pounding is severe; both humble the virtues.

9. But everything emerges more fragrantly and more perfectly from the furnace of blazing love. This flame not only humbles the virtues but even alters them, changes them into a new look and makes more spiritual what were already spiritual. The myrrh of continence, the incense of prayer, and the humble awareness of all one's virtues represented by the perfumer's powder, all these produce a countenance more serene and a look more pleasing, when they issue from this smithy's forge. Indeed the pestle and mortar of contrition is good, but firing in the forge is better. The perfumer's powder is fragrant, but the smoke surpasses it. For something more fragrant and more spiritual is represented by smoke than by powder. Therefore the bride, aglow with some gift of a blazing word in the Bridegroom's embrace, melts from perfumer's powder into finer wisps of smoke, from the dust of humbled virtues into the smoke of glory. What do you think her arrival will be like, when her ascent is so delightful? What is her destination when she ascends in such beauty? How great is the place of delights for which he arranges these ascents? Perhaps it is the bed of the Beloved. For to that especially the bride should aspire. Yes, obviously it is, as the next verse shows: 'Behold the carriage of Solomon, surrounded by sixty of the bravest men of Israel'.* Beautiful is the plan, that she should come

2 Co 12:1-7.

Sg 3:7.

from one little bed to another, from her own, from the chamber of her mother, to the carriage of her Solomon. No less appropriate is the variety which interlaces these delights with deeds of bravery, and that Solomon should surround his carriage with such a strong guard. But let us now check the reins of our galloping word, and devote a new sermon to a new verse with the aid of our Lord Jesus Christ, who lives and reigns for ever and ever. Amen.

NOTES TO SERMON FIFTEEN

1.   After a few introductory sentences to his brethren, *fratres,* G. continues throughout in the second person singular: *Attende . . . .*
2.   Leclercq, *Otia Monastica,* 108:35.
3.   Lam p. 170, n. 3; pp. 189-90, nn. 127, 131.
4.   Reading *corpulentae* for *torpulentae* with Mab.; see *corpulenta* in par. 6.
5.   G. writes *de ore,* Vulg. *de naribus.*
6.   Ws 2:2; G. writes *afflatus* and *scintillae;* Vulg. *flatus* and *scintilla.*
7.   Reading *sauciam* with Migne, for *sanctam* of Mab.

ABBREVIATIONS

ABR	*American Benedictine Review.* Newark, New Jersey, 1950-.
ASOC	*Analecta Sacri Ordinis Cisterciensis; Analecta Cisterciensia.* Rome, 1945-.
CC	Corpus Christianorum series. Turnhout, Belgium, 1953-.
CF	Cistercian Fathers Series. Spencer, Mass., Washington, D.C., Kalamazoo, Mich., Cistercian Publications, 1970-.
CS	Cistercian Studies Series. Spencer, Mass., Washington, D.C., Kalamazoo, Mich., Cistercian Publications, 1969-.
CSt	*Cistercian Studies.* Chimay, Belgium, 1961-.
Cîteaux	*Cîteaux: Commentarii cistercienses; Cîteaux in de Nederlanden.* Westmalle, Belgium, 1950-.
Coll.	*Collectanea o.c.r.; Collectanea cisterciensia.* Rome, 1934-.
de Lubac	De Lubac, Henri, *Exégèse Médiéval.* Paris, Aubier, 1959-64.
DSp	*Dictionnaire de Spiritualité,* Paris, 1932-.
Dion	*Oeuvres Complètes de Saint Bernard,* V:1-319, Latin text and French tr. of Gilbert of Hoyland, P. Dion. Paris: Vivès, 1873.
E	Epistle of Gilbert of Hoyland, cited by number and paragraph.
Flor.	*Sermones super Cantica Canticorum, Editio princeps* [of Gilbert of Hoyland]. Florence, Nicolaus Laurenti, 1485.
G.	Gilbert of Hoyland.
Gilson	Gilson, Etienne, *The Mystical Theology of Saint Bernard,* tr. A. H. C. Downes. London: Sheed and Ward, 1940.
Lam	M. Jean Vuong-dinh Lam, 'Le Monastére: Foyer de Vie Spirituelle d'après Gilbert de Hoyland' and 'Les observances monastiques: instruments de Vie Spirituelle d'après Gilbert de Hoyland', Coll. 26 (1964) 5-21, 169-199.
Leclercq	Leclercq, Jean, *The Love of Learning and the Desire for God: a study of monastic culture,* N.Y.: Fordham Press, 1961.

Miquel   Miquel, Pierre, 'Les Caractères de l'expérience religieuse d'après Gilbert de Hoyland', Coll. 27 (1965) 150-159.

Morson   Morson, John, 'The English Cistercians and the Bestiary', *Bulletin of John Rylands Library* 39 (1956) 146-172.

MS   *Mediaeval Studies.* Toronto, 1939–.

R.   Roger of Byland, 'Lac Parvulorum', ASOC 7 (1951) 218-231.

RAM   *Revue d'Ascétique et de Mystique.* Toulouse, 1920–.

RB   *St. Benedict's Rule for Monasteries.* Tr. Leonard Doyle, Collegeville: Liturgical Press, 1948. *La règle de S. Benoît.* Sources chrétiennes 181-183, ed. Adalbert de Vogüé (1972).

R. Ben.   *Revue Bénédictine.* Maredsous, Belgium, 1899-1910; 1911–.

S   Gilbert of Hoyland, *Sermons on the Canticle,* cited by number and paragraph.

SAn   *Studia Anselmiana* series. Rome, 1933–.

SBOp   *Sancti Bernardi Opera,* ed. J. Leclercq, C. H. Talbot, H. M. Rochais. Rome: Editiones Cistercienses, 1957–.

SC   Bernard of Clairvaux, *Sermons on the Song of Songs.* SBOp 1-2, tr. Kilian Walsh, The Works of Bernard of Clairvaux, CF 4, 7, [31, 40].

SMC   *Studies in Medieval Culture.* Kalamazoo, Mich., 1964–.

T   Gilbert of Hoyland, Ascetical Treatise, cited by number and paragraph.

Talbot   Talbot, C. H., 'A Letter of Roger, Abbot of Byland', ASOC 7 (1951) 218-231.

VCH   *The Victoria History of the Counties of England,* ed. William Page. II, *A History of Lincolnshire,* 22. The Abbey of Swineshead, pp. 145-46.

Vulg.   Vulgate.

White   White, Terence Hanbury, *The English Bestiary.* New York: Putnam, 1960.

Psalms have been cited according to the Vulgate enumeration. Abbreviations and nomenclature conform to that of the Jerusalem Bible.

A SELECTED BIBLIOGRAPHY

A Lapide, Cornelius. *Commentaria in Scripturam Sacram,* re-ed., Augustine Crampon. Paris: Vivès, 1860.

Blaise, Albert. *Corpus Christianorum Continuatio Medieualis, Lexicon Latinitatus Medii Aevi.* Turnhout: Brepols, 1975.

Bouyer, Louis. *The Cistercian Heritage,* tr. Elizabeth A. Livingstone, Westminister, Md.: Newman, 1958.

Buhot, Jacqueline. 'L'Abbaye Normande de Savigny'. *Moyen Age,* 46 (1936) 1-19, 104-121, 178-190, 249-272.

Cabassut, A., Olphe-Gaillard M., 'Cantique des cantiques au Moyen Age.' DSp 2 (1953) 101-102.

——— 'Une dévotion médiévale peu connue: la dévotion à Jésus notre Mère'. RAM 25 (1949) 234-245.

Chatillon, Jean. 'Cordis Affectus au Moyen Age'. DSp 2 (1953) 2287-2300.

——— 'Hic, ibi, interim'. RAM (1949) 194-199.

Cheney, C.R. 'Les Bibliothèques cisterciennes en Angleterre au XIIe siècle'. *Mélanges de Saint Bernard.* Dijon (1953) 375-382.

Chenu, M.D. *La théologie au douzième siècle.* Paris, 1957.

Cloes, H. 'La systematisation théologique pendant la 1ère moitié de XIIe siècle'. *Ephemerides Theologicae* 34 (1958) 277-328.

Colombas, G.M. 'Paradis et vie angélique, Le sens eschatologique de la vocation chrétienne'. *Spiritualité monastique.* Paris, 1961.

Costello, Hilary, 'Gilbert of Hoyland'. *Cîteaux* 27 (1976) 109-121.

Déchanet, J.M. 'Amor ipse intellectus est'. *Revue du Moyen Age Latin* 1 (1945) 349-374.

——— 'La contemplation au XIIè siècle'. DSp 2 (1953) 1948-66.

——— 'Les fondements et les bases de la spiritualité bernardine'. *Cîteaux* 4 (1953) 292-313.

De Clerck, E. 'Droits du démon et nécessité de la Rédemption'. RTAM 14 (1947) 32-64.

—— 'Questions de sotériologie médiévale'. RTAM 13 (1946) 150-184.

Delatte, Paul. *The Rule of Saint Benedict,* tr. Justin McCann. London: Burns and Oates, 1921.

Delfgaauw, P. 'An approach to saint Bernard's sermons on the Song of songs'. Coll. 23 (1961) 148-161.

—— 'La lumière de la charité chez S. Bernard'. Coll. 18 (1956), 42-69, 306-320.

De Lubac, H. *Exégèse médiévale: Les quatre sens de l'Ecriture.* Paris: Aubier, Coll. *'Théologie',* 1959-64.

Didier, J.C. 'L'ascension mystique et l'union mystique par l'Humanité du Christ selon saint Bernard.' *La vie spirituelle, Supplément* 5 (1930) 140-155.

Dimier, A. 'Les concepts de moine et de vie monastique chez les premiers Cisterciens'. *Studia Monastica* 1 (1959) 399-418.

—— 'Ménagerie Cistercienne' and 'Héraldique Cistercienne'. *Cîteaux* 24 (1973) 5-30, 267-282.

—— 'Observances monastiques'. ASOC 11 (1955) 149-198.

Dugdale, G. *Monasticon Anglicanum.* London: 1846-1855.

Dumeige, Gervais. 'Dissemblance'. DSp 3 (1957) 1330-43.

Dumont, C. 'L'équilibre humain de la vie cistercienne d'après le bien-heureux Aelred de Rievaulx'. Coll. 18 (1956) 177-189.

Dumontier, M. *Saint Bernard et la Bible.* Paris, 1953.

Foreville, Raymonde, 'Gilbert de Sempringham'. DSp 6 (1967) 374-375.

Gilson, Etienne, *The Christian Philosophy of Saint Augustine,* tr. L.E.M. Lynch. London: Gollancz, 1961.

—— *History of Christian Philosophy in the Middle Ages.* New York: Random House, 1954.

—— *The Mystical Theology of Saint Bernard.* Tr. A. H. C. Downes. London: Sheed and Ward, 1955.

Hallam, H. E. *Settlement and Society.* Cambridge U. Press, 1965.

Hallier, Amédée. *The Monastic Theology of Aelred of Rievaulx,* tr. Columban Heaney, CS2. Spencer, Mass., 1969.

Hill, Bennet D. *English Cistercian Monasteries and their patrons in the Twelfth Century.* Urbana: U. of Illinois Press, 1968.

Histoire Littéraire de la France. Edd. Benedictines of St. Maur and L'Institut des Inscriptions et Belles Lettres. Paris: Imprimerie Nationale, 1733-19--; 'Gilbert de Hoylandia', 13 (1814) 461-69.

Ioannis de Forda. *Super extremam partem cantici canticorum sermones CXX,* edd. Edmond Mikkers and H. Costello. *CC Continuatio Mediaeualis* 17-18. Turnhout: Brepols, 1970.

Javelet, Robert, 'Contemplation et vie contemplative aux VIe-XIIe siècles'. DSp 2 (1953) 1929-1948.

—— 'Exercises spirituels dans le Haut Moyen Age'. DSp 4 (1961) 1905-1908.

—— 'L'extase chez les spirituels du XIIe siècle'. DSp 4 (1961) 2113-2120.

—— 'Image et Ressemblance aux 11e et 12e siècles'. DSp 7 (1971) 1425-1434.

—— 'Intelligence et amour chez les auteurs spirituels du XIIe siècle'. RAM 37 (1961) 273-290, 429-450.

—— *Psychologie des auteurs spirituels du XIIe siècle*. Strassbourg 1959.

—— *Saint Bernard mystique*. Paris, 1948.

Knowles, David. *The English Mystical Tradition*. New York: Harper Torchbook, 1961.

—— *The Episcopal Colleagues of Archbishop Thomas à Becket*. Cambridge University Press, 1951.

—— *The Monastic Order in England*. Cambridge University Press, 1950.

—— *The Nature of Mysticism*. New York: Hawthorne, 1966.

—— *The Religious Orders in England,* 3 vols. Cambridge University Press, 1950.

Knowles, David, C.N.K. Brooke, Vera C.M. London, *The Heads of Religious Houses: England and Wales, 940-1216*. Cambridge U. Press, 1972.

Knowles, David and R. Neville Hadcock. *Medieval Religious Houses in England and Wales*. New York: Longmans, Green, 1953.

Knowles, David, and J.K.S. St. Joseph. *Monastic Sites from the Air*. Cambridge University Press, 1952.

Lambert, M. 'La date de l'affiliation de Savigny et de la Trappe à l'Ordre de Cîteaux'. Coll. 3 (1936) 231-233.

Lebreton, M. 'Christ and the christian faith according to St. Bernard'. *Cîteaux* 12 (1961) 105-119.

—— 'Recherches sur les principaux thèmes théologiques traités dans les sermons du XIIè siècle'. RTAM 23 (1956) 5-18.

Leclercq, Jean. 'Disciplina'. DSp 3 (1957) 1291-1302.

—— 'Les écrits de Geoffroy d'Auxerre, Appendices, II: La première rédaction des Sermones in Cantica de Gilbert de Hoyland'. *Revue Bénédictine* 62 (1952) 289-290.

—— 'Ecrits monastiques sur la Bible aux XIe–XIIIe siècles'. MS 15 (1953) 95-106.

—— 'Etudes sur le vocabulaire monastique du moyen âge', SAn 48 (1961).

—— 'Le genre épistolaire au moyen âge'. *Revue du Moyen Age latin,*

2 (1955).

—— *The Love of Learning and the Desire of God,* tr. Catherine Misrahi. New York: Fordham University Press, 1961.

—— 'Monachisme et pérégrination du IXe au XIIe siècle'. *Studia Monastica* 3 (1961) 33-52.

—— *Otia Monastica.* SAn 51 (1963).

Leclercq, Jean, François Vandenbroucke, Louis Bouyer. *The Spirituality of the Middle Ages.* London: Burns and Oates, 1968.

Lekai, Louis. *The White Monks.* Our Lady of Spring Bank, Okauchee. Wis.: Cistercians, 1953.

—— *The Cistercians: Ideals and Reality.* Kent, Ohio: Kent State Univ. Press, 1977.

Loomis, Roger Sherman. *The Grail, from Celtic Myth to Christian Symbol.* New York: Columbia U. Press, 1963.

Marié, G. 'Familiarité avec Dieu, Courant bénédictin et cistercien'. DS 5 (1962) 50-53.

Manrique, A. *Annales Cistercienses,* 4 vols. Lyons, 1642-1649.

Merton, L. 'Action and contemplation in St. Bernard', Coll. 15 (1953) 26-31, 203-216; 16 (1954) 105-121.

—— 'La doctrine de l'image chez saint Bernard'. *Ephemerides Theologicae* 23 (1947) 70-129.

—— 'Le principe de l'ordination dans la théologie spirituelle de S. Bernard'. Coll. 8 (1946) 178-216.

Mikkers, E. 'De vita et operibus Gilbert de Hoylandia'. *Cîteaux* 14 (1963) 33-43, 265-279.

—— 'Les sermons inédits de Jean de Ford sur le Cantique des cantiques'. Coll. 5 (1938) 250-261.

Miquel, Pierre. 'Les Caractères de l'Expérience Religieuse d'après Gilbert de Hoyland'. Coll. 27 (1965) 150-159.

Morson, John. 'The English Cistercians and the Bestiary'. *Bulletin of the John Rylands Library* 39 (1956) 146-170.

Migne, J.P., ed. *Patrologia Graeca.* Paris: 161 vols., 1857-1876. The volume number precedes the colon; the column number follows it.

—— *Patrologia Latina.* Paris: 222 vols., 1841-1864. The volume number precedes the colon; the column number follows it.

Prayers and Meditations of St. Anselm, tr. Benedicta Ward. Harmondsworth: Penguin, 1973.

Le règle de saint Benoît. Sources chrétiennes 181-183. Ed. Adalbert de Vogüé. Paris: Cerf, 1972.

Reypens, Leonce. 'Connaissance mystique de Dieu, au 12e et 13e siècles.' DSp 3 (1957) 829-901.

Riedlinger, H. 'Gilbert v. Hoyland.' *Lexikon für Theologie und Kirche,*

B. IV (1960) 890.

Robert, A., Tournay, R., Feuillet, A. *Le cantique des Cantiques*. Paris: Gabalda, 1963.

The Rule of Saint Benedict. Edited by Justin McCann. London: Burns Oates, 1952.

St. Benedict's Rule for Monasteries. Tr. Leonard Doyle, Collegeville: Liturgical Press, 1948.

Sancti Bernardi Opera, edd. J. Leclercq, C.H. Talbot, H.M. Rochais. Rome: Editions Cistercienses, 1957–.

Sancti Bernardi Opera Omnia, ed. Jean Mabillon. Milan: Gnocchi, 1690, rpt. 1850-52.

Smalley, Beryl. *The Study of the Bible in the Middle Ages*. Oxford, 1952, 2nd ed.

Squire, Aelred. *Aelred of Rievaulx: a study*. London, SPCK, 1969.

Talbot, C.H. 'A Letter of Roger, Abbot of Byland'. ASOC 7 (1951) 219-221.

Valléry-Radot, Irénée. 'La Queste del Saint Graal'. Coll. 17 (1956) 3-20, 199-213, 321-332.

Van den Bosch, Amatus. 'Intelligence de la Foi chez Saint Bernard'. *Cîteaux* 8 (1957) 85-108.

Vandenbroucke, François. 'Direction spirituelle en Occident, au Moyen Age'. DSp 3 (1957) 1083-1098.

Vuong-dinh-Lam, M. Jean. *Doctrine Spirituelle de Gilbert de Hoyland, d'après son Commentaire sur le Cantique des cantiques*. Diss., Rome: Collegium Anselmeanum, 1963.

—— 'Le Monastère: foyer de vie spirituelle d'après Gilbert de Hoyland', Coll. 26 (1964) 5-21.

—— 'Les Observances Monastiques: instruments de vie spirituelle d'après Gilbert de Hoyland', Coll. 26 (1964) 169-199.

—— 'Gilbert de Hoyland', DSp 6 (1967) 371-374.

White, Terence Hanbury. *The English Bestiary*. New York: Putnam, 1960.

William of St Thierry. *Exposition on the Song of Songs*. CF 6. Spencer, Mass., 1970.